Jay XO

Preface

The law of tort is built on cases. This represents a challenge to the learning capacity of the student, there is so much information to be digested. A case book is an aid to that digestion. Cases are presented here in an explanatory style and in an accessible form. The student is warned that he would be wise to read some of the cases in the original; he will then get a feel for the fabric of the law of tort. However, life is short and tort is long so some assistance is necessary. Cases here are presented in short form but with some a lengthier, more explanatory style is adopted.

Interspersed in the text are some moot questions. They are designed to test the student's understanding of what he has read. To answer a problem the student is required first to identify the issues involved; second he must cite the relevant cases; third he is to apply those cases to the facts given; finally he should give a reasoned solution. In short the student has to decide who sues whom and for what.

JL
August 1995

Contents

Table of cases

1 Forms of action

1.1 The Judicature Act 1873 abolished forms of action

Konskier v Goodman (1928)

Defendants were builders who, in the course of building elsewhere, obtained permission to pull down and rebuild a chimney of a house; the defendants left rubbish on the roof which subsequently choked a gully which later led to flooding in the basement. In the meantime the original occupier had leased the premises to the plaintiff and his goods were damaged by the flooding. At first instance the plaintiff succeeded in *negligence*. The Court of Appeal reversed this, holding that there was no duty owed to *him* as he had no interest in the premises at the time when permission was granted (a pre-*Donoghue v Stevenson* decision).

However, the Court of Appeal went on to hold that the plaintiff succeeded in *trespass* even though his case had been pleaded and argued in negligence. The defendants were guilty of a trespass in allowing rubbish to remain after a reasonable time; their licence had ended and plaintiff was in possession at the time of the flooding.

Per Scrutton LJ:

> A plaintiff is not now found to state the legal effect of the facts on which he relies; he is only bound to state the facts themselves and we cannot see that the defendant has suffered any injustice in the way of being shut out from giving evidence which he might have given if the action had been treated as an action for trespass.

1.2 An amendment in pleading is not permitted if it would involve adducing fresh evidence

Esso v Southport Corporation (1956)

The plaintiff was the owner of a foreshore polluted by oil from an Esso tanker which had run aground after a steering failure; the ship's master had loosed oil in order to save the lives of the crew. Trial judge had held that the Corporation was entitled to succeed in trespass or nuisance and in negligence but that the defendant succeeded on the grounds of necessity. The Court of Appeal reversed that decision, holding that *res ipsa loquitur* applied (see Chapter 2) and that Esso had failed to explain why the steering had gone wrong. That decision was in turn reversed by the House of Lords.

Held that adherence to the pleadings was not 'pedantry or mere formalism'; the function of the pleadings was to give fair notice of the case to be met. Evidence in that case was concerned only with the negligence alleged and that concerned the *navigation* of the vessel; there was no notice of any other cause of action such as sending a vessel to sea in an unseaworthy condition which would have involved fresh evidence. Esso had had no notice of *that*.

1.3 Pleadings define the issues before the court

Farrell v Secretary of State for Defence (1980)

The plaintiff was the widow of a man shot by soldiers. At trial the allegations were concerned with the conduct of the *soldiers*. In the Court of Appeal there were allegations against those who had *planned* the operation and a new trial was ordered.

Held (HL) that there should be *no* new trial and that verdict for the defendant should stand.

2 Negligence

2.1 Duty of care

2.1.1 There is a duty of care not to injure one's neighbour

Donoghue v Stevenson (1932)

The plaintiff drank ginger beer given to her by a friend and manufactured by the defendants; the drink was contaminated by the decomposed remains of a snail and the plaintiff argued that she had suffered injury as a result of seeing and drinking that. The House of Lords held 3–2 that although there was no contractual duty owed to her by the manufacturers, nevertheless they did owe her a legal duty to take care that the bottle did not contain noxious matter.

Per Lord Atkin:

(1) You must take reasonable care to avoid acts or omission which you can reasonably foresee would be likely to injure your neighbour. Who, then, in law is my neighbour? The answer seems to be (2) Persons who are so closely and directly affected by my act that I ought reasonably to have them in contemplation as being so affected when I am directing my mind to the acts or omissions which are called into question.

Home Office v Dorset Yacht Co (1970)

A yacht owned by the plaintiff was boarded and damaged by Borstal boys who were under the supervision of servants of the defendant; the plaintiff alleged that there was inadequate supervision of the boys; the defendant pleaded that the Borstal officers did not owe the plaintiffs a duty of care.

Held (4–1 HL) that such a duty of care *did* exist. The principle of *Donoghue v Stevenson* was directly applicable for the damage suffered was the very kind of thing which the officers should have foreseen. General rule was that one man was under no duty of controlling another so as to prevent his damaging a third; however here there was a *special relationship* between the two which *did* give rise to such a duty to the third.

Cf *Hill v Chief Constable of West Yorkshire* (1988).

Hill v Chief Constable of West Yorkshire (1988)

A 20-year-old student was murdered by Peter Sutcliffe – the 'Yorkshire Ripper' who had committed 12 other murders in the same area. Her mother sued the police on behalf of her daughter's estate for alleged negligence in failing to catch Sutcliffe earlier than they did.

Held (HL) that the claim involved failure to control another person so as to prevent him from doing harm to others; the general rule denied a duty of care in such a situation and there was insufficient proximity between the parties to take the case out of that general rule.

Per Lord Keith of Kinkel:

> All householders are potential victim of an habitual burglar, and all females those of an habitual rapist. The conclusion must be that although there existed reasonable foreseeability of likely harm to such as Miss H if Sutcliffe were not identified and apprehended, there is absent from the case any such ingredient or characteristic as led to the liability of the Home Office in the *Dorset Yacht* case. Nor is there present any additional characteristic such as might make up the deficiency. The circumstances of the case are therefore not capable of establishing a duty of care owed towards Miss H by the West Yorkshire police.

HL further held that public policy was a reason why an action for damages should not lie against the police. *Per* Lord Keith of Kinkel:

> The general sense of public duty which motivates police forces is unlikely to be appreciably reinforced by the imposition of such liability so far as concerns their function in the investigation and suppression of crime ... In some instances the imposition of liability may lead to the exercise of a function being carried on in a detrimentally defensive frame of mind.

2.1.2 There must be a special relationship when damage is caused by a third party

Perl v Camden LBC (1983)

The defendant owned an unoccupied basement flat which was not secured to prevent admission by intruders; thieves entered the flat and through the party wall gained admission to the plaintiff's premises.

Held (CA) that in the absence of a special relationship, there was no duty of care on the defendant to prevent a third party from gaining access to the plaintiff's property from the defendant's property.

Per Waller LJ:

> A very high degree of foreseeability is required if liability is to be imposed on a person for the acts of an independent third party.

Stansbie v Troman (1948)

A decorator left a house unlocked in order to go out to obtain more wallpaper; the householder had specifically requested him not to leave the house unlocked; whilst he was out the house was burgled.

Held (CA) that the decorator was liable for the loss; in view of the specific request by the householder and his breach of that undertaking, what happened subsequently was his responsibility.

Smith v Littlewoods (1987)

The defendants purchased a cinema with a view to its demolition and replacing it with a supermarket; cinema was closed and some preliminary work was done. For a fortnight thereafter cinema remained empty and unattended. Debris accumulated outside and two attempts were made to start fires but neither the defendants nor the police were informed. Then a fire was started in the cinema and seriously damaged two adjoining properties. Owners of those properties claimed damages on the grounds of the defendant's negligence. Trial judge awarded damages, judgment was overruled on appeal and the plaintiffs appealed to the House of Lords on the basis that it was reasonably foreseeable that if a cinema were left unsecured, children would be attracted to the building, would damage it by fire which would then spread to the plaintiff's property.

Held (HL) that the defendants were under a *general* duty of care to see that the condition of their premises did not constitute a source of danger to neighbouring property. Whether, within that duty, there was a *specific* duty to prevent damage from fire resulting from vandalism, depended on whether it was reasonably foreseeable that if owner took no action to keep premises lockfast before demolition, they would be set on fire. In view of the facts, especially the short period of time and that two previous fires attempts were unreported and so unknown, the events which occurred were *not* reasonably foreseeable by the defendants. Accordingly they owed *no* such specific duty to the plaintiffs.

Per Lord Mackay:

> When the word 'probable' is used in this context [where the injury or damage was caused by an independent human agency] in the authorities it is used as indicating a real risk as distinct from a mere possibility of danger.

Per Lord Goff:

> That there are special circumstances in which a defender may be held responsible in law for injuries suffered by the pursuer through a third party's deliberate wrong doing, is not in doubt.

Q Bill Sykes escapes from prison and for several days lives rough. He then breaks into the house of Widow Twanky and steals food. Advise the widow.

Q Gormless buys fireworks on 1 November and stores them in his garden shed. Artful Dodger breaks into the shed on 4 November and sets light to the fireworks. The fire spreads to a neighbour, Glum, and destroys his house. Consider legal liability.

2.1.3 The law of England may in certain circumstances not recognise the existence of a duty of care

Ashton v Turner (1980)

The plaintiff and the defendant participated in a burglary; the plaintiff was injured when the defendant was driving the getaway car.

Held a duty of care did not exist between the parties during the course of burglary and during the course of subsequent flight.

2.1.4 A duty of care does arise when the defendant assumes a task

Wheeler v Copas (1981)

Defendant lent a ladder to his builder, the ladder was inadequate and broke.

Held the defendant liable in negligence. A voluntary bailee had a duty to take reasonable care to see that what he was lending was, so far as reasonable care could, be made safe for the purpose for which it was bailed.

2.1.5 Master is under no duty to protect his servants property from a dishonest act of a third party

Deyong v Shenburn (1946)

The plaintiff was engaged by the defendant to play in his pantomime; he agreed to rehearse in a place chosen by the defendant; during rehearsal the plaintiff's clothing was stolen from the dressing room.

Held (CA) that although the defendant was careless, no action in negligence lay as there was no duty of care.

Q Would it have made a difference if the plaintiff had been required to *reside* in a place of the defendant's choosing?

McCarthy v Daily Mirror (1949)

Here the Court of Appeal held that where employee's property was stolen from printing works – the plaintiff's locker was broken into – there was a possible breach of the statutory duty under Factory Act 1937 s 43 to provide 'adequate and suitable accommodation for clothing not worn during working hours'. Matter was remitted to county court judge for his determination of this factual point.

2.1.6 Plaintiff must establish that there was a duty of owed to him

Bourhill v Young (1943)

The plaintiff, a distant bystander, suffered nervous shock at seeing the result of an accident caused by the defendant's negligence.

Held (HL) that although the defendant owed a duty of care to other road users, he did not owe such a duty to the plaintiff because, on the facts, her presence there was not foreseeable.

2.1.7 Various criteria for establishing a duty of care

Home Office v Dorset Yacht Co (1970)

Per Lord Reid:

> *Donoghue v Stevenson* may be regarded as a milestone, and the well known passage in Lord Atkin's speech should I think be regarded as a statement of principle. It is not to be treated as if it were a statutory definition. It will require qualification in new circumstances. But I think the time has come when we can and should say that it ought to apply unless there is some justification or valid explanation for its exclusion.

Anns v Merton (1978)

Per Lord Wilberforce:

> First one has to ask whether, as between the alleged wrongdoer and the person who has suffered damage, there is sufficient relationship of proximity or neighbourhood such that, in the reasonable contemplation of the former, carelessness on his part may be likely to cause damage to the latter, in which case a *prima facie* duty of care arises. Secondly, if the first question is answered affirmatively, it is necessary to consider whether there are any considerations which ought to negative, or to reduce or limit, the scope of the duty or the class of person to whom it is owed or the damages to which a breach or it may give rise.

Note *Murphy v Brentwood* [1990].

Held Anns v Merton to be wrongly decided and not followed, see p 34.

Leigh & Sullivan Ltd v Aliakmon Shipping (1986)

Per Lord Brandon:

> I do not think that Lord Wilberforce in formulating the two questions which he did formulate in his speech in *Anns* case, was intending them to be used as a means of reopening issues relating to the existence of a duty of care long settled by past decisions.

Sutherland Shire Council v Heyman (1985) ALR

Per Brennan J:

> It is preferable, in my view, that the law should develop novel categories of negligence incrementally and by analogy with established categories rather than by

a massive extension of a *prima facie* duty of care restrained only by indefinable considerations which ought to negative or to reduce or limit the scope of the duty or the class of person to whom it is owed.

Approved by the House of Lords in *Murphy v Brentwood* (1990).

Caparo Industries v Dickman (1990)

Per Lord Bridge:

I think the law has now moved in the direction of attaching greater significance to the more traditional categorisation of distinct and recognisable situations as guides to the existence, the scope and the limits of the varied duties of care which the law imposes.

Q Consider how, if at all, these separate pronouncements can be reconciled.

2.1.8 No duty of care owed by classification society

The Nicholas H (1995)

In 1986 the owners of a vessel entered into an agreement to load bulk cargoes in South America and to ship them to Italy and the Black Sea. The goods were loaded under bills of lading incorporating the Hague Rules. Two weeks after embarking, the vessel anchored off Puerto Rica, having reported a crack in her hull to US coastguard. Vessel was inspected at anchor by a surveyor acting for the vessel's classification society, NKK. Ship entered harbour and certain repairs were carried out. Surveyor recommended that vessel continue its voyage but the temporary repairs to be further examined and dealt with after the discharge of her cargo. Vessel sailed from port but on the following day vessel reported that repairs had failed and a few days later the ship sank with a total loss of cargo.

Cargo owners sued ship owner as carrier and NKK for damages. Claim against ship owner was settled by payment of a proportion of loss. NKK was pursued for balance of claim. Classification societies perform a public function, often employed by governments to check that vessels comply with state regulations. In performing a private function such societies set their own standards and are employed by ship owners and insurance companies to check whether vessels comply with those standards.

Held (HL 4–1) that a duty of care should not be imposed on marine classification societies. In imposing a duty of care it was necessary to consider whether the negligent party foresaw or should reasonably have foreseen the damage; the nature of relationship between the parties, whether it was sufficiently close to supporting a duty of care; finally whether in all the circumstances it would be fair, just and reasonable to impose a duty of care.

Held it would be unfair, unjust and unreasonable towards classification societies because they acted for the collective welfare and, unlike ship owners, they would not have the benefit of any limitation provisions. *Lesser* injustice would be done by *not* recognising a duty of care.

HL approved a *dictum* of Saville LJ:

These cases are not irreconcilable. What they do is to demonstrate that in differing circumstances the same or similar factors may take on a different significance.

2.2 Breach of a duty of care

2.2.1 The standard is based upon the reasonable man

Blyth v Birmingham Waterworks (1856)
An unprecedented frost had caused mains water to freeze.

Held that there was no negligence as water mains had been laid at the conventional depth.

Per Baron Alderson:

Negligence is the omission to do something which a reasonable man, guided upon those considerations which ordinarily regulate the conduct of human affairs, would do, or doing something which a prudent and reasonable man would not do.

2.2.2 Where a transaction necessarily involves a certain skill, it is no defence that the person who undertook the transaction did not possess it

Wells v Cooper (1958)
The defendant householder had fitted a door handle; later the door handle came off in the hand of the plaintiff, a visitor.

Held (CA) that the defendant owed a duty of care to the plaintiff. However the defendant *was* justified in carrying out the work himself as he was an amateur carpenter of some experience. Thus there was no breach of the duty of care.

Q Miss Happ wishes to have her ears pierced; she goes to Flash, a High Street jeweller; within two days of Flash piercing her ears, she has an ear infection. Advise Miss Happ.

2.2.3 There should be a degree of care commensurate with the risk created

Paris v Stepney BC (1951)
The House of Lords held that an employer had a duty to provide goggles for a one eyed man even though it was *not* necessary to provide goggles for a workman with two eyes. Total blindness is a much greater risk than the loss of one eye.

2.2.4 Importance of the object to be achieved is a factor

Marshall v Osborne (1983)
The defendant policeman drove a police car in pursuit of a stolen car in which the plaintiff was travelling; in the process of arrest the plaintiff was injured by the police car.

Held (CA) that claim in negligence failed; the defendant was not guilty of want of care in all circumstances.

2.2.5 Regard must be had to the practicability of precautions

Latimer v AEC (1953)
A factory became flooded and oil was loosed on to the floors, rendering them slippery; sawdust was laid to cure this but one small area was left uncovered due to insufficiency of sawdust; the plaintiff slipped on uncovered area, injuring himself.

Held (HL) that the defendant was not under a duty to close the factory; this was too onerous a precaution in view of the small risk involved.

2.2.6 Defendant may be required to adapt his conduct

Defendant will be required to adapt his conduct to allow for any peculiarities of plaintiff either known – *Paris v Stepney* – or reasonably foreseeable.

Haley v LEB (1964)
The blind plaintiff fell into a ditch dug by the defendant; precautions taken by the defendant were sufficient for a sighted person.

Held (HL) there was a duty of care owed to *all* persons using the highway and this included blind persons; their presence on the highway was reasonably foreseeable; there was a breach of this duty to the plaintiff as barrier provided was not suitable for a blind person. The burden of providing a suitable barrier was not too great. Post Office provided portable fence for its excavations and that barrier was effective for blind *and* sighted persons. LEB could and should have done something similar.

Q Mutt is deaf; he fails to hear a warning shouted by Brown, a lorry driver who is about to reverse; Mutt is then run down by the lorry. Can Mutt sue Brown?

2.2.7 Defendant may escape liability if he has acted in accordance with general practice

Roe v Ministry of Health (1954)
An anaesthetist was employed by the defendant; in 1947 he administered to the plaintiff a spinal anaesthetic; the anaesthetic was contained in an ampoule which had been kept in phenol; because of an invisible crack in the ampoule the anaesthetic was contaminated with the phenol. As a result

of the spinal injection the plaintiff was paralysed; had the phenol been coloured the contamination would have been apparent.

Held (CA) that the anaesthetist was not negligent in failing to take the additional precaution of colouring the phenol in 1947; the danger of invisible cracks was not drawn to the attention of the medical profession until 1951.

Bolam v Friern HMC (1957)

The plaintiff suffered a fracture whilst he was undergoing electro-convulsive therapy; the doctor had failed to give a muscle relaxant before the treatment. There were differences of practice regarding this.

Held that a doctor was not negligent if he had acted in accordance with a practice accepted as proper by a reasonable body of medical men skilled in that particular art. A man was not negligent if he were acting in accordance with that practice merely because there was a body of opinion which would take a contrary view. By jury verdict, the defendants held *not liable*.

Bolam was approved by the House of Lords in *F v West Berkshire Health Authority* (1989).

Clark v Maclennan (1983)

Plaintiff suffered from stress incontinence after the birth of her child; *one* month after the birth an operation was performed by the defendant to relieve the condition; normal practice was not to operate until at least *three* months after the birth; operation was a failure.

Held the *evidential* burden of showing he was not in breach of his duty was on the defendant; the departure from the general practice had not been justified by the defendant and thus the plaintiff's claim succeeded.

Sidaway v Bethlehem Royal Hospital (1985)

The plaintiff was operated on by a surgeon employed by the defendants. The operation was conducted without negligence but as a result she suffered damage to the spinal cord; there was a risk of less than 1% that this could happen; she was not informed of this risk when she consented to the operation. She sued the defendants on the ground that the surgeon failed to inform her of the risk.

Held (HL) that her claim failed.

Per Lord Bridge:

The issue whether non-disclosure in a particular case should be condemned as a breach of the doctor's duty of care is an issue to be decided primarily on the basis of expert medical evidence, applying the *Bolam* test.

Q *Sidaway* did not apply *Bolam* but *extended* it. Discuss this proposition.

2.2.8 *Res ipsa loquitur* (the very happening of the accident may be evidence of negligence)

Cassidy v Ministry of Health (1951)

The plaintiff was operated upon, by servant of the defendant, for two stiff fingers; on post operational inspection it was discovered that he was then suffering from four stiff fingers. Plaintiff's claim succeeded.

Per Denning LJ:

> I went into hospital to be cured of two stiff fingers. I have come out with four stiff fingers ... Explain it if you can.

2.2.9 The legal burden of proof remains on the plaintiff but there is an evidential burden placed on the defendant, ie a burden to adduce evidence

Ward v Tesco (1976)
The plaintiff, a customer of the defendant, slipped and fell due to 'spillage' on the floor.

Held (CA) 2–1, that in the *absence of explanation by the defendant* as to how long the spillage had remained there, the plaintiff was entitled to succeed in her claim for negligence.

Per Lawton LJ:

> Such burden of proof as there is on the defendant in such circumstances is evidential, not probative. The trial judge thought that *prima facie* this accident would not have happened had the defendant taken reasonable care. In my judgment he was justified in taking that view because the probabilities were that the spillage had been on the floor long enough for it to have been cleared up by a member of the staff.

In *Roe v Ministry of Health* (1954), where the plaintiff was paralysed as a result of a spinal anaesthetic, the Court of Appeal held that *res ipsa loquitur* applied. However, the claim failed as the defendant was able to explain how the accident happened *without* negligence on his part.

Colvilles v Devine (1969)
The plaintiff, an employee of the defendant, was injured in a violent explosion.

Held (HL) that the maxim was applicable. Defendant's explanation gave the *probable* cause of the explosion, ie that the oxygen supply had been contaminated by dirt particles. However that explanation was *no* defence as the defendant had adduced no evidence to explain that contamination and thus their own explanation was *not* consistent with no negligence on their part.

Per Lord Donovan:

> It was for the appellants (the defendant) to show that the accident was just as consistent with their having exercised due diligence as with their having been negligent. In that way the scales which had been tipped in the respondent's (the plaintiff's) favour by the doctrine of *res ipsa loquitur* would once more be in balance, and the respondent would have to begin again and prove negligence in the usual way.

Q Speed overturns a hired van while driving down a motorway; there was no other vehicle involved. Advise Speed.

3 Causation

3.1 Plaintiff must prove a causal connection between his damage and the defendant's breach of duty

Barnett v Chelsea HMC (1968)

The deceased presented himself at the defendant's casualty department with a history of vomiting; he was told to see his own doctor; five hours later he died of arsenic poisoning.

Held there was a duty of care and further there was a breach of that duty as the plaintiff should have been examined, admitted and treated. However, the claim *failed* because on the evidence, there was no chance of the specific antidote being administered before the time of the death; deceased would have died *anyway*, treatment or no treatment.

3.2 Same test applies in breach of statutory duty

McWilliams v Sir William Arroll Ltd (1962)

The deceased was killed falling from a tower which he was erecting; he was not wearing a safety belt; if he had been he would not have been killed. Evidence was that if safety belts had been supplied they would not have been worn.

Held (HL) that the claim failed. Defendant was entitled to say that if safety appliances had been supplied they would not have been worn; the plaintiff would not have worn safety belt anyway, supply or no supply.

3.3 There may be *two* causes for the plaintiff's injury

McGhee v National Coal Board (1972)

The plaintiff claimed damages in respect of his employer's fault in failing to provide adequate washing facilities to remove dust from his body before leaving his place of work.

Held (HL) that his dermatitis resulted from two causes: (1) exposure to dust; (2) subsequent omission to wash before leaving. *Only* (2) was the fault of the defendant but nevertheless the plaintiff's claim succeeded; the defendant's breach of duty had materially increased the risk of injury and this was a material contribution to the injury.

Hotson v East Berkshire AHA (1987)

Here the plaintiff fell from a tree and injured his hip; there was a negligent delay in his treatment and subsequently he suffered from a permanent disability in his hip. The evidence was that although he might have had the disability *anyway*, there was a 25% chance that he might have recovered had he been treated promptly.

Held (HL) that he was not entitled to 25% of his damages; the rule remained that the plaintiff has the burden of establishing – on balance of probabilities – that his personal injury was caused by the defendant's negligence.

Q How can these two cases be reconciled?

4 Remoteness of damage

4.1 The rule in *The Wagon Mound*

A person is only responsible for consequences intended or probable; a consequence is probable when a reasonable man would have foreseen it.

The Wagon Mound (No 1) (1961)

The plaintiff was repairing a ship using welding equipment; the defendant negligently released fuel oil 200 yards away; it was not reasonably fore-seeable that the oil would ignite; it did so 60 hours later and the resultant fire damaged the plaintiff's wharf. Trial judge held the defendant was liable because *some* damage was foreseeable, the slipways were in fact rendered temporarily unusable. Applying the direct test – *Re Polemis* (1920) – the fire was the direct physical result of releasing the oil. The decision was reversed by JCPC which expressly *disapproved* of *Re Polemis*.

Held it was not consonant with current ideas of justice that for an act of negligence, however slight, the actor should be made liable for all consequences, however unforeseeable, so long as they were 'direct'.

4.2 The same test is used for liability in nuisance

The Wagon Mound (No 2) (1966)

The plaintiff was the ship-owner whose vessel had been destroyed by the fire at the wharf; trial judge held – on hearing different evidence from *The Wagon Mound No 1* – that the risk of fire was foreseeable but *not* reasonably foreseeable.

Held (JCPC) that fire *was* a reasonable foreseeability; the ship's activity was unlawful; a properly qualified and alert Chief Engineer would have realised that there was a real risk of fire and that that should have been in the mind of a reasonable man in the position of the defendant's servants; the defendant held liable in public nuisance.

4.3 Plaintiff can recover when the ultimate injury is similar in type

Where the ultimate injury is similar in type to the original injury, it is deemed to be foreseeable even though the precise sequence of events, leading to the plaintiff's damage, is not.

Hughes v Lord Advocate (1963)

Post office employees left unattended an open manhole, covered by a canvas shelter and surrounded by red warning lights. Plaintiff, aged eight, played with a lamp while within the shelter; lamp fell into the hole and the plaintiff was badly burnt in the resultant explosion.

Held (HL) that it was negligent to have left the manhole and lamps unattended; it was foreseeable that a child would be burnt in consequence. It mattered not that the burn*ing was the result of an *explosion* which could not, even long after the event, be satisfactorily explained.

4.4 Plaintiff cannot recover when source of injury is unforeseeable and damage is of an entirely different kind

Doughty v Turner (1964)

The plaintiff was standing by a cauldron of molten metal; the defendant's servants had let slip into the tank an asbestos cover; it was then unknown that an explosion would result from the effect of heat on asbestos; an explosion did result two minutes later and the plaintiff was injured.

Held (CA), following *The Wagon Mound*, the defendant was not liable because the eruption which injured the plaintiff was unforeseeable by a reasonable man at the time when the accident happened. The risk of splashing was foreseeable but what happened was an accident of an entirely different kind caused by an unexpected factor, viz the instability of asbestos at high temperature.

Q Why did *Hughes* recover damages for a burn caused by an unforeseeable explosion whereas *Doughty* did not recover for a burn caused by a foreseeable splash?

Tremain v Pike (1969)

The plaintiff was employed as a herdsman on the defendant's farm where there were rats; the plaintiff contracted Weill's disease through contact with rodent urine.

Held the plaintiff could not recover as Weill's disease was a *remote* possibility – in 1967 there had only been eight cases nationally. The *kind* of damage suffered by the plaintiff was entirely different from the effect of a rat bite or food contamination; Weill's disease was the only rat-induced disease not caused by one or other.

4.5 Intervention of third party may be defendant's responsibility

If defendant's negligence creates the opportunity for a third party to injure plaintiff, then defendant will be responsible for the intervention if the act of the third party was reasonably foreseeable.

See *Home Office v Dorset Yacht Co* (1970) above.

Lamb v Camden LBC (1981)

Per Oliver LJ:

> There may be circumstances in which the Court would require a degree of likelihood amounting almost to inevitability before it fixes a defendant with responsibility for an act of a third party over whom he has and can have no control.

In 1972 plaintiff let her house while she was abroad. A year later council contractors breached the water main outside plaintiff's house; foundations were undermined and house was rendered unsafe; the tenants left and plaintiff's furniture was moved into storage. While the house was empty, awaiting repair, some squatters moved in but were evicted and the house boarded up. In 1975 squatters again moved in and caused extensive damage. Defendant *admitted* liability in nuisance for damage to the house but denied liability in negligence for malicious damage caused by squatters.

Held (CA) that damage was too remote: a reasonable man wielding his pick could *not* have reasonably foreseen that puncturing a water main would, a year and more later, fill plaintiff's house with unwanted guests.

Per Lord Denning:

> Looking at the question as one of policy, I ask myself: whose job was it to do something to keep out the squatters? And if they got in, to evict them? To my mind the answer is clear. It was the job of the owner of the house, Mrs Lamb, through her agents.

Haynes v Harwood (1935)

A defendant negligently left horses unattended; a boy threw stones at them and they bolted. The plaintiff, a policeman, was injured while attempting to prevent them from running down children.

Held (CA) that the defendant was liable as what had happened was reasonably foreseeable.

Philco v Spurling (1949)

The defendant mistakenly delivered some celluloid to the plaintiff; typist employee of the plaintiff stubbed out her cigarette on the celluloid; in the resultant fire the plaintiff's premises were damaged.

Held (CA) that in the *absence* of evidence that typist set light to the celluloid intentionally, the defendant was liable as it was reasonably foreseeable that, if the celluloid were left where it was, such damage might arise from the act of a *foolish* person. Had the stubbing of the cigarette been malicious, then the proximate cause of the danger would have been the conscious act of another's volition which would not have been foreseeable.

4.6 *The Wagon Mound* has not changed the rule that a negligent tortfeasor takes his victim as he finds him – 'the egg-shell skull' rule

Smith v Leach Brain (1961)

The deceased was splashed by molten metal, as a result of an unsafe system of work; the splash burned his lip which was in a pre-malignant condition; as a result of the wound, cancer developed in the tissue and deceased died of cancer three years later.

Held that the 'egg-shell skull' principle was concerned with the situation where a *particular type* of injury could be foreseen – in that case the burn – and the question then what was the *measure* of damage, and *that* depended on the character and constitution of the victim.

Q Can a lip burn and cancer of the lip be treated as different measures of the same type of injury?

Robinson v The Post Office (1974)

The plaintiff slipped when he was using an oily ladder and lacerated a leg; his doctor gave him an anti-tetanus injection to which he was allergic; as a result the plaintiff developed encephalitis, a *rare* consequence.

Held (CA) that the defendant was liable for the brain damage, the injection was not a *novus actus interveniens*. The principle that a defendant must take the plaintiff as he finds him involved that a wrongdoer ought reasonably to foresee that, as a result of his wrongful act, the victim may require medical treatment; he is then, subject to the principle of *novus actus interveniens*, liable for the consequences of that treatment although he could not reasonably foresee those consequences.

Q Would it have made any difference had the doctor in *Robinson* been negligent?

4.7 Financial frailty is to be distinguished from physical weakness

Liesboch Dredger v SS Edison (1933)

A dredger was sunk by the negligence of the Edison; owners of the dredger were too poor to buy a replacement and had to hire a substitute to carry out an existing contract; it would have been cheaper to buy.

Held (HL) that the plaintiff's damages were limited to the cost of the purchase and to damages for loss of hire between the sinking and the date when a replacement *would* have been put into service.

Dodds Properties v Canterbury CC (1980)

The plaintiff's property was damaged by the defendant's negligence in 1970; repairs were not carried out until 1978 when judgment was given for the plaintiff.

Held (CA) that it was *reasonable* in view of all the circumstances – the plaintiff's poverty *and commercial* prudence – for the repairs to have been delayed. The result was that 1978 prices and not 1970 prices were to be taken into account when assessing damages.

4.8 There may be successive acts of negligence

Knightley v Johns (1982)

D1 negligently overturned his car in a road tunnel; the plaintiff, a police constable, was ordered by his inspector, D4, to ride the wrong way down the tunnel as D4 had forgotten to close it; the plaintiff crashed into D2; there was a breach of standing order, muddle and confusion. D1 *conceded* his negligence but pleaded that the *cause* of the accident was the negligence of others.

Held (CA) that the inspector was negligent in not closing the tunnel and in ordering the plaintiff to execute a dangerous manoeuvre; his negligence was a *new* cause disturbing the sequence of events leading from D1 overturning his car. D4's negligence had been the real cause of the plaintiff's injuries. Accordingly then, D3, the police authority, and D4 were liable, *not* D1 and D2.

5 Contributory negligence

5.1 Rules of apportionment

5.1.1 Maritime Conventions Act 1911 s 1
A court apportions loss according to the degree in which each vessel is at fault. Where in all the circumstances it is not possible to establish different degrees of fault, liability is apportioned equally.

5.1.2 Law Reform (Contributory Negligence) Act 1945 s 1(1)
This provides that contributory negligence shall *not* defeat a plaintiff's claim but that the plaintiff's damages shall be reduced to such extent as the court thinks *just* and *equitable*, having regard to the plaintiff's *share* in the responsibility for the damage.

The Miraflores (1967)
The House of Lords *held* that, despite the difference in the wording, the basis of apportionment is the same under either Act; the criteria is *fault* although both causative potency and blame worthiness have to be considered.

5.2 Negligence of each party must be a cause of the accident

Jones v Livox (1954)
The plaintiff rode on the tow bar at back of vehicle, contrary to orders; the defendant's servant ran on to the back of the vehicle.

Held (CA) the plaintiff guilty of contributory negligence, assessed at 20%; his decision to ride on the back was a *cause* of the accident; it did not matter that he was crushed rather than thrown off.

5.3 Plaintiff suffering greater injury

If, as a result of his contributory negligence, the plaintiff suffers greater injury than he otherwise would have sustained, then his entitlement to compensation should reflect that fact.

Froom v Butcher (1975)

The Court of Appeal *held* that failure to wear a seat belt – not then a legal requirement – was contributory negligence. The question was, what was the cause of the accident? The damage was caused in part by the defendant's bad driving and in part by the failure of the plaintiff to wear a seat belt – a prudent precaution. Where damage would have been prevented the Court of Appeal thought damages should be reduced by 25%; where damage would have been a good deal less severe, by 15%. On the particular facts the Court of Appeal assessed the contributory negligence at 20%.

5.4 Causal connection must be established by the defendant

Owens v Brimmell (1976)

The parties had been out drinking together; the defendant drove the plaintiff home; as a result of driver's admitted negligence the car crashed and the plaintiff was severely injured.

Held that the failure to wear a seat belt was *not* contributory negligence because the defendant had failed to establish, on balance of probabilities, that the plaintiff's injuries were increased by that failure; the plaintiff's head hit the fascia and did not go through the windscreen.

However, accepting a lift when the plaintiff knew the defendant was intoxicated *was* contributory negligence on the plaintiff's part as he had exposed himself to danger unreasonably. Trial judge assessed the figure at 20%.

5.5 The dilemma principle

Where the defendant's negligence has put the plaintiff in a dilemma, the plaintiff is not to be blamed if, in the agony of the moment he has taken a wrong step.

Jones v Boyce (1816)

The plaintiff, reasonably fearing for his own safety, jumped from a runaway coach and broke his leg.

Held it was reasonable for him to have jumped as his apprehension of the *alternative* danger – that the coach might overturn – was a reasonable one in the circumstances.

Sayers v Harlow UDC (1958)

The defendant was negligent in inviting the plaintiff to use one of their public lavatories; the cubicle had no inside door handle with the result that the plaintiff was locked in.

Held (CA) that she was entitled to attempt to get out and the defendant was responsible for the injury sustained when she fell in her attempt to climb out. However, her damages were reduced by 25% because, by putting her weight on such a fragile fitting as a toilet roll, she had contributed to her fall.

5.6 A child must be given special consideration

Gough v Thorne (1966)

The plaintiff, a 13-year-old pedestrian, relied entirely on lorry driver's signal beckoning her to cross; she crossed the road and was hit by the defendant who was driving too fast.

Held (CA) she was not contributorily negligent in relying entirely on lorry driver's signal.

Per Lord Denning MR:

A very young child cannot be guilty of contributory negligence. An older child may be, but it depends on the circumstances.

Q William, aged 15, chases a football across a quiet street. Flash, driving at 60 mph, hits him. Plod drives into the back of Flash. Consider the respective liabilities.

6 Nervous shock

6.1 Liability is for shock, it is not an action to recover damages for grief

Hinz v Berry (1970)

A family was picnicking in a lay-by; the plaintiff saw her husband killed and her children injured by the defendant's out-of-control car. Defendant appealed against an award of £4,000 damages for nervous shock.

Held (CA) that the award – although a high one – should stand.

Per Lord Denning MR:

> Somehow or other the court has to draw the line between sorrow and grief for which damages are *not* recoverable and nervous shock and psychiatric illness for damages which *are* recoverable.

Per Lord Pearson:

> Compensation 'should only be for that additional element which has been contributed by the shock of witnessing the accident and which would not have occurred if she had not suffered *that* shock.

6.2 Witness and victim must have some mutual bond which need not be parenthood

Dooley v Cammell Laird (1951)

The plaintiff was a crane driver; he feared for the safety of his *fellow* workers when he saw the rope carrying the load snap and load fall into the hold of ship.

Held he could recover damages for his subsequent nervous shock.

6.3 The 'egg-shell skull' principle applies to cases of nervous shock

Brice v Brown (1984)

The plaintiff suffered unforeseeably severe nervous shock.

Held that the plaintiff had to establish first that the circumstances of the accident *caused* nervous shock. Second, that nervous shock was reasonably foreseeable by the defendant as a natural and probable consequence; for *that* purpose the plaintiff was assumed to be a person of normal disposition and phlegm. Third, the plaintiff *then* could recover damages for consequences not dissimilar *in kind*, whether or no they were reasonably foreseeable.

In the event the plaintiff recovered £26,000 damages for nervous shock sustained after sitting in a taxi with her daughter and taxi was involved in a collision; the daughter was injured in collision which was caused by the taxi driver's negligence. The damages were much higher than usual in an action for nervous shock; the plaintiff was entitled to damages for the cost of care at home, calculated to be £2,600 per annum; the plaintiff was then given a multiplier of 10, thus damages amounted to £26,000.

6.4 There is sufficient proximity if the plaintiff comes upon the immediate aftermath of the accident

McLoughlin v O'Brien (1982)
The plaintiff's family were injured and one member killed in an accident caused by the defendant's admitted negligence; she was told *one hour later* of the accident; she then went to the hospital and saw the injuries; the plaintiff subsequently suffered nervous shock as a result of what she had seen and what she had been told.

Held (HL) that the plaintiff was entitled to recover damages from the defendant because even though she was not at or near the scene of the accident, the nervous shock suffered by her in the immediate aftermath was a reasonably foreseeable consequence of the defendant's negligence.

6.5 Reasonable foreseeability of nervous shock is, by itself, not sufficient

Alcock v Chief Constable of South Yorkshire (1992)
Relatives of the deceased and injured saw horrific sights of the disaster at the football stadium of Hillsborough. Eight out of 10 saw the sights through the medium of television; two brothers were present at the ground but were some distance from the actual disaster. Defendants admitted liability in respect of the deaths and physical injuries but denied a duty of care in relation to nervous shock.

Held (HL) that all 10 claims failed. First, regarding the brothers, the plaintiff's action failed because although there were sufficient ties of relationship, the actual evidence failed to show sufficient love and affection. Second, three other plaintiffs had these ties but only saw the scenes on television; by a code of ethics no identifiable victims were shown; thus there was no sudden assault on the nervous system. Third, there was no 'immediate aftermath' because visiting the mortuary for the purpose of identification was not sufficiently immediate, psychiatric illness must be caused by *shock*. The House of Lords declined to fix particular relationships, such as husband and wife, for this type of action. However, sufficient closeness of tie was to be proved by the plaintiff.

Per Lord Ackner:

> There may be circumstances where the element of direct visual perception may be provided by witnessing the actual injury to the primary victim on *simultaneous* television.

6.6 Psychiatric damage not limited to witnessing a personal injury

Attiah v British Gas (1987)

Plaintiff engaged defendants to install central heating in her house. While defendants were engaged in the work plaintiff returned home one afternoon to see smoke pouring from the house. She telephoned the fire brigade; by the time the fire was brought under control four hours later, house and contents were extensively damaged. Defendants admitted liability for the fire and settled plaintiff's claim for damage to house and contents but disputed her claim for nervous shock; this claim was tried as a preliminary issue.

Held (CA) that damages for psychiatric damage were *not* limited to witnessing a personal injury as a consequence of defendant's negligence. Damages could be recovered where plaintiff witnessed the destruction of his home and possessions as a result of defendant's negligence provided plaintiff proved psychiatric damage and not merely grief, sorrow or emotional distress. Such psychiatric damage must have been reasonably foreseeable. That was a question of *fact* to be decided at trial. In the result then CA declined to strike out plaintiff's claim.

Per Bingham LJ:

> Her claim is accordingly one for what in the authorities and literature have been called damages for nervous shock. Judges have in recent years become increasingly restive at the use of this misleading and inaccurate expression, and I shall use the general expression 'psychiatric damage', intending to comprehend within it all relevant forms of mental illness, neurosis and personality change.

Per Woolf LJ:

> I cannot conceive that, if the injury which the plaintiff alleges that she suffered was a foreseeable consequence of the defendant's negligence, there could be any overriding policy reason for preventing her recovering damages. As I have already pointed out, she could well have sustained physical injuries as well as the psychiatric injuries of which she complains when she would have been

entitled to damages and in my view there can be no reason of policy for distinguishing between the two types of injury.

Q Miss Chance returns home to find her house in flames due to the negligence of British Gas; she suffers nervous shock at the sight. Advise her. Would it make any difference if she had a history of mental illness?

6.7   A distinction is drawn between primary and secondary victims

Page v Smith (1995)
Plaintiff involved in a collision with the defendant; plaintiff was unhurt in the collision but the accident caused him to suffer the onset of myalgic encephalomyelitis (ME) from which he had suffered for about 20 years but which was then in remission. Recrudescence of ME was likely to prevent him from working again.

Held (HL 3–2) applying principle that defendant has to take the victim as he finds him, a negligent driver sued for damages arising out of a motor vehicle accident caused by him, was liable for damages for nervous shock suffered by the *primary* victim of the accident. It was only necessary if personal injury of *some* kind to that person was reasonably foreseeable as a result of the accident. Plaintiff was *not* required to prove that injury by nervous shock was reasonably foreseeable. It was irrelevant that defendant could not have foreseen that plaintiff had an egg shell personality.

Per Lord Lloyd:

> In cases involving nervous shock, it is essential to distinguish between the primary victim and secondary victims. In claims by secondary victims the law insists on certain control mechanisms, as a matter of policy, to limit the number of potential claimants. Thus the defendant will not be liable unless psychiatric injury is foreseeable in a person of normal fortitude. These control mechanisms have *no* place where the plaintiff is the *primary* victim.

7 Economic loss

7.1 Plaintiff cannot recover for pure economic loss

Weller v Foot and Mouth Disease Research Institute (1965)
The plaintiff alleged that the defendant had negligently released a virus and that in consequence there was an outbreak of foot and mouth disease with the consequent loss of markets; the plaintiff, an auctioneer, suffered financial loss.

Held that even on the assumption of facts most favourable to the plaintiff, he could not recover. A duty of care which arose from a risk of direct injury to persons or property, was owed only to those whose person or property might foreseeably be injured by a failure to take care. On the facts duty of care was owed to *owners* of cattle in the neighbourhood, not to auctioneers of cattle. Thus no duty was owed to the plaintiff by the defendant.

7.2 Where the plaintiff has suffered physical damage, he can recover the economic loss that flows from that damage

Spartan Steel v Martin (1972)
The plaintiff manufactured stainless steel; whilst digging up the road, the defendant damaged the electric cable which supplied electricity to the plaintiff; there was a power failure which prevented the plaintiff's furnace from working. Plaintiff claimed (a) damage to material in furnace (b) loss of profit thereon (c) loss of profit through period of power cut. Defendant *admitted* negligence and *admitted* (a) and (b) but claimed (c) was economic loss for which they were not liable.

Held (CA 2–1) that the plaintiff could not recover (c) because there was economic loss *independent* of the physical damage.

7.3 Liability is denied where the plaintiff's loss results from physical damage to another's property

Electrochrome v Welsh Plastics (1968)
The defendant's servant negligently damaged a fire hydrant and the supply of mains water was stopped for several hours; as water was essential to the plaintiff's business, his factory ceased to operate for one day.

Held the plaintiff could not recover the financial loss from the defendant whose duty of care was owed to the owner of the hydrant, not to the plaintiff, the owner of the factory.

7.4 Liability of manufacturer of defective product

Manufacturer of a defective product will only be liable in tort in respect of damage caused to *other* property, not for defects in the product itself.

Muirhead v International Tank Specialities Ltd (1986)

The plaintiff planned to buy lobsters in the summer when they were cheap; they were to be kept in a tank and sold at Christmas when they were dear. Tank was installed by X and, by subcontract between X and the defendant, the water in the tank was to be aerated by pumps manufactured by the defendant; the pumps failed and the lobsters died. X became bankrupt so the plaintiff's contractual remedy against him was worthless.

Held (CA) that the defendant had been negligent and the plaintiff recovered damages flowing from the death of the lobsters because damage of that type was reasonably foreseeable by the manufacturers. However *no* damages were awarded to represent money spent on the purchase of the pumps and on attempts to repair them. That was pure economic loss, there was no damage to the pumps, they simply did not work.

Per Goff LJ:

> The buyer, if he seeks to recover damages for purely economic loss arising from defects in the goods, must on the law as it stands, look to his immediate vendor and not the ultimate manufacturer for his remedy.

7.5 Close proximity may be sufficient for recovering economic loss

Junior Books Ltd v Veitchi (1982)

The plaintiff engaged X to build a factory for them; the plaintiff nominated the defendant as subcontractors to lay a special floor; later faults developed and the plaintiff sued the defendant for the cost of replacement and for consequential economic loss during this period of replacement. Defendant pleaded that there was no action in tort.

Held (HL) that there was sufficient proximity between producer of defective article and user, despite the absence of a contractual relationship. The proximity was such that it fell only just short of a direct contractual relationship. Claim succeeded.

Per Lord Roskill:

> Scots and English Law extends the duty of care beyond a duty to prevent harm being done *by* faulty work to a duty to avoid such faults being present in the work itself.

In *Muirhead per* Goff LJ:

On the facts in *Junior Books* it was considered by the majority of House of Lords that the nominated subcontractor has assumed a direct responsibility to the building owner. Voluntary assumption of responsibility, in circumstances akin to contract, was the basis of liability in the *Hedley Byrne* case which Lord Roskill regarded as relevant in *Junior Books* ...

It is, I think safest for this court to treat *Junior Books* as a case in which, on its particular facts, there was considered to be such a very close relationship between the parties, that the defenders could, if the facts as pleaded were proved, to be held liable to the pursuers.

Q The decision in Junior Books has been much criticised. Why?

7.6 Plaintiff's proprietary interest necessary

House of Lords reaffirmed the necessity of the plaintiff's proprietary interest in the physically damaged property to support a claim for financial loss.

Leigh & Sullivan v Aliakmon Shipping (1986)

The buyers agreed to buy from sellers a quantity of steel coils which were to be shipped from Korea to UK. Steel was badly stowed and was damaged *en route*. Before damage was discovered sellers tendered bill of lading for payment but buyers were unable to make payment. There was a *variation* of contract, the effect of which was that buyer had assumed the risk of damage to the goods without becoming the holder of the bill of lading. The buyer sought to sue the ship owner for the damage to the goods. The Court of Appeal had held there was no contract between ship owners and buyers.

The House of Lords affirmed principle that a person could not claim in negligence for loss caused to him by reason of loss or damage to property unless he had either *legal* ownership or a *possessory* title to the property at the time when loss or damage occurred. There were no policy reasons why, in the case of c i f or c and f buyer of goods to whom the risk had passed but not title, there should be an exception to the rule that *only* the legal owner or person having possessory title to goods could sue in negligence for damage to them. Claim in negligence thus failed.

Per Lord Brandon:

Under the usual cif or c and f contract the bill of lading issued in respect of the goods is endorsed and delivered by the seller to the buyer against payment by the buyer of the price. When that happens, the property in the goods passes from the sellers to the buyers on or by reason of such endorsement, and the buyer is entitled by virtue of s 1 of the Bills of Lading Act 1855, to sue the ship owners for loss or damage to the goods on the contract contained in the bill of lading. The remedy so available to the buyer is adequate and fair to both parties, and there is *no need* for any parallel or alternative remedy in tort for negligence.

But see now *Carriage of Goods by Sea Act 1992* s 2(1).

8   Negligent misstatement

8.1   Special relationship

A special relationship is sufficient to establish a duty of care.

Hedley-Byrne v Heller (1964)

The plaintiff was anxious to learn whether a client X was financially stable; the plaintiff's bank was asked to obtain this information for him; the bank obtained a reference from the defendant who were X's bankers. Reference was favourable but was given 'without responsibility'; X was in fact in financial difficulty and shortly afterwards went into liquidation; in consequence the plaintiff suffered a loss of £17,000.

Held (HL) that the defendant's disclaimer of responsibility was a good defence; however *but for* this disclaimer there would have been a duty of care. No exhaustive definition of this necessary special relationship was given but Lord Devlin termed it 'equivalent to contract'. Thus it was made clear that there would still be no liability for casual statements made on social occasions. But where inquirer is trusting the other to exercise a reasonable degree of care and where the other – as a reasonable man – knows that his skill or judgment are to be relied on, then a duty of care does arise.

Anderson v Rhodes (1967)

The plaintiff, a potato dealer, asked the defendant wholesaler about the credit-worthiness of X; the defendant, who stood to gain commission on the business, replied carelessly, 'They are all right'; the plaintiff lost money on giving credit to X in reliance on that statement.

Held the defendant was liable as this was a business transaction, the nature of which made clear the gravity of the enquiry.

Q Bill Sykes wishes to join the local tennis club. The club secretary wishes to obtain a reference and approaches Nancy who says 'Bill is all right.' Soon after becoming a member, Bill Sykes runs off with the club silver. Advise the secretary.

8.2   JCPC took a narrow view of *Hedley-Byrne*

Mutual Life v Evatt (1971)

The plaintiff, a policy holder in the defendant insurance company, sought their advice regarding another company's financial soundness; the advice given was incorrect and the plaintiff lost his money.

Held 3–2 that *Hedley-Byrne* should be understood as being restricted to advisers who carried on the business or profession of giving advice of the kind sought. *Anderson v Rhodes* was left on the basis that it was a situation where the adviser had a financial interest in the transaction on which he gave advice. There was a notable dissenting advice from Lords Reid and Morris and it was not followed by the Court of Appeal in *Esso v Marden* below.

8.3   There may be concurrent liability in contract as well as in tort

Esso v Marden (1976)
The plaintiff induced the defendant in 1963 to enter into a tenancy agreement (thus prior to Misrepresentation Act 1967); the defendant relied on the plaintiff's estimate of potential turnover; this forecast was by then out of date; in 1964 the plaintiff offered the defendant a new agreement because of the losses but these continued and in 1966 the plaintiff claimed possession, money owed and mesne profits.

Held (CA) first that the plaintiff's statement to the defendant was a *collateral warranty* and that warranty was broken. Secondly in any event the statement was a negligent statement under *Hedley-Byrne*; in the case of a professional man, the duty to use reasonable care arose not only in contract but was imposed by the law *apart* from contract and was therefore actionable in tort. Damages were recoverable from 1963 and also from the new agreement in 1964; the defendant had tried to mitigate his loss and the effect of the original misstatement was still there – it laid a 'heavy hand' on all that followed.

8.4   A legal duty is to be distinguished from a moral duty

Argy v Lapid (1977)
The plaintiff was a tenant of the defendant who agreed to insure buildings against fire under a 'block' scheme whereby the plaintiff paid a proportionate part of the premium; later the defendant's interest in the property was taken over by X who effected their own insurance; the result was that from January 1973 the plaintiff was uninsured; the defendant did not tell the plaintiff of the change in insurance arrangements; in October 1973 the plaintiff's property was destroyed by fire.

Held the plaintiff's claim under *Hedley-Byrne v Heller* failed although there was a special relationship between two parties. There was no legal – cf moral – duty on the part of the defendant to tell the plaintiff of the change in the insurance position.

Moorgate Mercantile v Twitching (1976)

The plaintiff was a hire purchase company which had hired a car to X; for some reason the agreement was not registered with the Hire Purchase Information Ltd, of which the plaintiff was a member; X sold the car to the defendant.

Held (HL) that the plaintiff *could* sue the defendant in conversion; there was no *duty* to register, thus the plaintiff was not estopped from asserting his own title by his failure to register his transaction.

8.5 There is less difficulty in establishing liability for careless statements causing physical injury

Clay v Crump (1963)

An architect was asked to inspect a wall; he said it was safe when it was not; it subsequently fell on the plaintiff workman, injuring him.

Held he was liable for his careless statement.

Q Presto while driving his car stops to seek help; a passer-by, Simon, tells him the road ahead is quite straight. Presto then drives on and crashes on an acute bend. What, if any, is the liability of Simon?

8.6 Physical injury must be distinguished from financial loss

Murphy v Brentwood (1990)

The plaintiff purchased, in 1970, a new semi-detached house from the construction company; it was built on an infilled site on a concrete raft to prevent damage from settlements. Defendant council referred plans to consulting engineers and on their recommendation the defendant passed plans under building regulations. In 1981 serious cracks appeared and in 1986 – unable to carry out repairs – the plaintiff sold house for £35,000 less than its market value in sound condition. He sued Council and obtained damages. The Court of Appeal held, following *Anns v Merton*, that council owed the plaintiff a duty of care and was in breach of that duty when it approved plans for a defective raft foundation. Council appealed.

Held (HL) that the local authority was *not* liable in negligence to building owner or occupier for the cost of remedying a dangerous defect in the building, which resulted from negligent failure of authority to ensure that building was designed or erected in conformance with approved standards, but which became apparent before defect caused physical injury. The damage suffered by the building owner or occupier in such circumstances was not material or physical damage but the purely *economic* loss of the expenditure incurred in rectification.

Per Lord Keith:

In my opinion it must be recognised that although the damage in Anns was characterised as physical damage by Lord Wilberforce, it was purely economic loss.

Held Anns v Merton wrongly decided and not followed. *Dutton v Bognor Regis* overruled. Appeal allowed.

Per curiam:

It is unrealistic to regard a building or chattel which has been wholly erected or manufactured and equipped by the *same* contractor as a 'complex' structure in which one part of the structure is regarded as having caused damage to the *other property* when it causes damage to another part of the *same* structure.

D & F Estates Ltd v Church Commissioners for England (1988)

D3 builders were the main contractors for the construction of a block of flats which were owned by D1. D3 engaged a subcontractor to carry out plastering work; they reasonably believed him to be competent but the work was carried out negligently. Plaintiffs were lessees and occupiers of a flat in the block. Fifteen years later the plaintiffs discovered plaster in their flat was loose. Plaintiff *inter alia* sued D3.

Held (HL) that the builders were not liable for the negligence of their subcontractor in carrying out the plastering because builder's *only* duty was to employ a competent plasterer which they had done. Law did not recognise any further duty.

In the absence of a contractual relationship between the parties, the cost of repairing a defect in a chattel or structure which was discovered before defect had caused personal injury or physical damage to other property, was not recoverable in negligence because the cost of repair was *pure economic loss* and not recoverable in tort. Thus builders were not liable whatever their vicarious liability.

8.7 Accountant's duty of care

JEB Fasteners v Bloom (1981)

Held that accountants to a company owed a duty of care to persons who were likely to take over the company and who would rely on the accounts. Defendant accountant was in breach of that duty as he had overvalued stock and had failed to inform the plaintiff of this in discussions prior to the plaintiff's take-over of the company. On the facts however, the plaintiff would have taken over the company *anyway*, thus there was no causal connection and the action failed.

The House of Lords considered the position of the accountant in *Caparo Industries v Dickman* (1990). The necessity of *proximity* was emphasised: (a) that the defendant *knew* his statement would be communicated to the plaintiff either as an *individual* or as a member of an *identifiable* class; and (b) that the plaintiff would be *very likely* to rely upon it for the purpose of deciding whether or not to enter on that transaction.

Per Lord Bridge:

> In *JEB* trial judge reached the conclusion that the duty could be derived from foreseeability alone ... I do not agree with this ... However the particular facts in *JEB* were sufficient to establish a basis on which the necessary ingredient of proximity to found a duty of care could be derived from the actual *knowledge* on the part of the auditors of the *specific purpose* for which the plaintiffs intended to use the accounts.

In *Caparo* the plaintiff had *bought* shares in F company; he had *owned* shares in the company and later *took over* the company. The House of Lords held that the auditor of a public company's accounts had *no* duty of care to members of the public at large buying shares – there was no proximity. Further there was *no* duty of care either to the shareholders *as such* or to them as *potential investors*.

Held the plaintiff's claim for financial loss failed.

Per Lord Bridge:

> I think the law has now moved in the direction of attaching greater significance to the more traditional categorisation of distinct and recognisable situations as guides to the existence, the scope and the limits of varied duties of care which the law imposes.

Q A trustee has advanced trust money on the certificate of a surveyor who had prepared it under a contract with the borrower, expressly that a mortgage might be arranged. There was an overvaluation. Advise the trustee.

8.8 There are cases of professional immunity

Rondel v Worsley (1967)

The House of Lords held that a barrister – despite *Hedley-Byrne* – is not liable for negligence in respect of his conduct of a case *in court*. This rule is based on public policy, particularly: (1) avoiding a 'trial of a trial'; (2) 'cab rank' rule of the Bar, a barrister is not allowed to refuse a brief; (3) *dual* function of counsel, he has a duty to the court as well as to his client; (4) general immunity of those engaged in judicial process; a solicitor *advocate* is also immune.

Ali v Mitchell (1978)

The House of Lords decided that there was no blanket immunity in respect of all 'paperwork'. The test was whether the particular paper work was so intimately concerned with the conduct of the case in court, that it could fairly be said to be a preliminary decision affecting the *way* that a case was to be conducted when it came to a hearing. Facts were that the plaintiff had been injured in a road accident; he consulted the defendant solicitor who then sought counsel's opinion; the opinion advised against suing a potential defendant. Next the plaintiff sued the solicitor in contract and the defendant served a Third Party Notice on counsel, claiming negligent advice.

Held (HL 3–2) that the Notice should *not* be struck out for disclosing no cause of action. *Per* Lord Salmon:

> In my opinion there is no such connection between the advice given in the present case and the conduct of a case in court. The advice given made it impossible for the plaintiff's unanswerable case to be heard in court. It was not even remotely connected with counsel's duty to the court or with public policy.

8.9 The immunity claimed must form part of a judicial process

Sutcliffe v Thakrah (1974)

The House of Lords held that an architect owed a duty of care to his client when issuing interim certificates for work done.

Held it was illogical to say, 'All persons carrying out judicial functions must act fairly, therefore all persons who act fairly are carrying out judicial functions.'

Arenson v Casson Beckman (1975)

The House of Lords held that a valuer, *unlike* an arbitrator, can be sued in negligence.

Per Lord Fraser:

> The main difference between an arbitrator and a valuer is that the arbitrator, like a judge, has to decide a dispute that has already arisen and he usually has rival contentions before him, while the mutual valuer is called in *before* a dispute has arisen, in order to avoid it.

Evans v London Hospital (1981)

The plaintiff, who had been charged with murder, could not sue in negligence the defendant pathologist whose report had formed the foundation of the prosecution of the plaintiff.

Per Drake J:

> It is essential that the immunity given to a witness should also extend to cover statements he made prior to the issue of a writ or commencement of a prosecution, provided that the statement is made for the purpose of a possible action or prosecution.

8.10 Liability is based on proximity

Yiani v Evans (1981)

A building society surveyor was held to have a duty of care to the purchaser of a house; the defendant surveyor *admitted* his survey was negligent in failing to report gross defects but denied a duty of care to the plaintiff purchaser.

Held there *was* such a duty, based on proximity; the defendant knew building society would rely on report and by their offer of a loan would pass on the valuation; the defendant knew that as a matter of practice the plaintiff would rely on that valuation and would not have an independent survey. Defendant's liability was not unlimited because the only party to whom he owed a duty of care was to the party *named* in building society's instructions to value.

Smith v Bush (1989)

Yiani was approved by the House of Lords. The plaintiff applied to a building society for a mortgage to enable her to purchase a house; the building society was under a statutory duty to obtain a written valuation report on the house; society instructed the defendant surveyor to inspect the house and to carry out a valuation. Plaintiff paid society a fee and signed an application form which contained a disclaimer to the effect that neither the society nor its surveyor warranted that the report and valuation would be accurate and they were supplied without any acceptance of responsibility. In reliance on that report, and without obtaining an independent survey, the plaintiff purchased the house. Defendant had observed that first floor chimney breasts had been removed but did not check to see whether chimneys were adequately supported. Eighteen months after purchase bricks from chimney collapsed and fell through roof causing considerable damage.

Held (HL) that a valuer who valued a house for a building society for the purpose of mortgage application, knowing that mortgagee probably, and mortgagor certainly, would rely on the valuation, owed a duty of care to *both* parties to carry out his valuation with reasonable skill and care. It made no difference by whom valuer was employed since he was discharging the duties of a professional man on whose skill he knew the purchaser would be relying. Fact that building society was acting under a statutory duty made no difference. Liability was *limited* to the purchaser of the house and did *not* extend to subsequent purchasers.

Per Lord Templeman:

> The contractual duty of a valuer to value a house for the Abbey National did not prevent the valuer coming under a tortious duty to Mrs Smith who was furnished with a report of the valuer and relied on the report.

The House of Lords held valuer *could* disclaim liability to exercise reasonable skill and care but disclaimer was subject to the Unfair Contract

Terms Act 1977 s 2(2) and therefore had to satisfy the requirement of *reasonableness* to be effective.

Held that it would not be fair or reasonable for mortgagees and valuers to impose on purchasers the risk of loss arising as a result of incompetence or carelessness on the part of valuers. It followed therefore the disclaimers were *not* effective to exclude liability for the negligence of the valuer.

8.11 Duty of care owed to intended beneficiary

Ross v Caunters (1979)

A disappointed legatee sued solicitor who had drawn up the will in question on the instructions of the testator; legacy failed because solicitor had negligently allowed the will to be attested by legatee's husband – Wills Act 1839 s 15.

Held the disappointed beneficiary could sue in tort for the financial loss because of the *high degree* of proximity.

White v Jones (1995)

Testator quarrelled with his two daughters, the plaintiffs; he executed a will cutting them out of his estate. Three months later he was reconciled with the plaintiffs; he sent a letter to his solicitors, giving instructions that a new will should be prepared, to include gifts of £9,000 each to plaintiffs. The solicitors received the letter but nothing was done. Finally steps were started to draw up a new will but testator died before he could be interviewed. CA had held plaintiffs were each entitled to damages of £9,000.

Held (HL 3–2) dismissing the appeal, that the solicitor *was* liable for the loss of the legacy, because the assumption of responsibility by the solicitor towards his client should be *extended* in law to an intended beneficiary since otherwise an injustice would occur because of a lacuna in the law; there would be no remedy for the loss caused by the solicitor's negligence *unless* intended beneficiary could claim. The extension was by analogy with established categories of relationships giving rise to a duty of care.

Per Lord Goff:

In my opinion, therefore, your Lordship's house should in cases such as these extend to the intended beneficiary a remedy under the *Hedley Byrne* principle by holding that the assumption of responsibility by the solicitor towards his client should be held in law to extend to the intended beneficiary who (as the solicitor can reasonably foresee) may as a result of the solicitor's negligence, be deprived of his intended legacy in circumstances in which neither the testator nor his estate will have a remedy against the solicitor.

Per Lord Browne-Wilkinson:

Save in the case of those rash testators who make their own wills, the proper transmission of property from one generation to the next is dependent on the due discharge by solicitors of their duties. Although in any particular case it may not be possible to demonstrate that the intended beneficiary relied upon the solicitor, society as a whole does rely on solicitors to carry out their will-making functions carefully. To my mind it would be unacceptable if, because of some technical rules of law, the wishes and expectations of testators and beneficiaries generally could be defeated by the negligent actions of solicitors without there being redress. It is only just that the intended beneficiary should be able to recover the benefits which he otherwise would have received.

8.12 Even where the defendant is obliged to make a statement, *Hedley-Byrne* may be applicable

Ministry of Housing v Sharpe (1970)

A landowner was refused permission to develop his land; he was paid compensation by the Ministry which registered a compensation notice in the local land charges register. Subsequently planning permission was granted and a prospective purchaser, who *would* have been liable to repay the compensation, received a clear certificate of search from that registry. The result was that the purchaser was free from this obligation and the Ministry suffered a loss; there had been negligence on the part of the local authority's employee.

Held (CA) that the employee was liable and the local authority vicariously liable. It did not matter that the certificate was not issued to the person injured.

9 Occupiers' liability

9.1 There is no statutory definition of 'occupier'

9.1.1 There may be more than one occupier at the same time

Fisher v CHT (1966)

The plaintiff was a servant of D3, a builder; D1 owned a club which included a restaurant operated by D2 under licence from D1; while the plaintiff worked on a ceiling he was injured by the negligence of D2. The Court of Appeal held that both D1 and D2 were occupiers and both were liable to their visitor. D3 was liable as the plaintiff's *employer*.

The House of Lords considered the point in *Wheat v Lacon* (1966). Facts were that the father of the Wheat family took them to an inn owned by the defendant; they were there as summer visitors; the defendant brewery, by agreement, permitted the manager and his wife, the Richardsons, to provide accommodation for such visitors. Father fell down an unlit and steep staircase situated in private part of the premises and was killed. The Court of Appeal had held that the widow's claim under Fatal Accidents Act 1846 failed as the brewery were not occupiers.

Held (HL) that they *were* occupiers through the occupancy of their servants. The test of *immediate* supervision and control was too narrow.

Per Lord Denning MR:

Whenever a person has sufficient degree of control over premises that he ought to realise that any failure on his part to use care may result in an injury to a person coming lawfully there, then he is an 'occupier' and the person coming there is his 'visitor'.

Per Lord Morris:

The general result of the agreement was that the respondents through their servant were in occupation of the whole of the premises. Both the respondents and the Richardsons were 'occupiers' and owed Mr Wheat a duty. The measure and content of that duty were not however necessarily the same in the case of the respondents and the Richardsons, eg suppose a mishap arose from the condition of the furnishings.

9.2 The Occupiers' Liability Act 1957

9.2.1 By s 1(2) a visitor is a person who would at common law have been treated as an invitee or licensee

By s 13(a) the occupier's duties apply not only to land and buildings but also to fixed and movable structures.

See *O'Connor v BTC* (1958) below.

9.3 The common duty of care

9.3.1 By s 2(1) an occupier of premises owes the same duty, the 'common duty of care', to all his visitors, except in so far as he is free to and does so extend, restrict, modify or exclude his duty to any visitor or visitors by agreement or otherwise

Section 2(2) defines the common duty of care: it is 'a duty to take such care as in all the circumstances of the case is reasonable to see that the visitor will be reasonably safe in using the premises for the purposes for which he is invited or permitted by the occupier to be there'.

9.3.2 Examples of the standard of care

Reffell v Surrey CC (1964)

The plaintiff was a schoolgirl who had put her hand through a glass swing door; for many years the defendant had known that the glass was insufficiently strong; new schools were fitted with toughened glass; the defendant's policy had been to replace the existing glass with toughened glass but only on breakage.

Held the safety of the pupil, a lawful visitor, had not been reasonably assured and that there was a breach of the common duty of care; the risk of the accident was reasonably foreseeable.

Watt v Herts CC (1969)

The plaintiff child injured himself when he crashed into a flint wall bounding a school playground; the presence of the flints increased the danger of a child hurting himself. The Court of Appeal held the defendant not liable – it is not every accident that a child suffers on school premises that will import liability. It was further held that more supervision by the school would not have made any difference, as a child playing, supervised or not, could still have fallen against the wall.

Q Tom and Jerry are playing in their school playground; they tumble against a railing which collapses; they suffer injury. The playground is unsupervised. Advise their parents

9.3.3 Once the plaintiff has come on to the premises as a lawful visitor, he will remain a visitor unless there is strong evidence to the contrary

Pearson v Coleman Bros (1948)

A little girl attended the defendant's circus as an invitee (pre-1957 case); in the interval she sought a ladies' lavatory; there was none; in her search for a place to relieve herself she went into a private part of the circus and was mauled by a lion.

Held (CA) that she *remained* an invitee and was thus able to recover damages.

Stone v Taffe (1974)

The plaintiff visited a public house managed by D1 and owned by D2; the plaintiff left at 1 am, no extension of licensing hours had been applied for; an exit staircase had been left in darkness and whilst descending the plaintiff fell and was killed.

Held (CA) that the plaintiff had come on to the premises as a visitor and *remained* a visitor because he was unaware that permission to be on the premises had expired at 10.30 pm. The unlit staircase was a breach of s 2(2) and the claim succeeded, subject to a finding of 50% contributory negligence.

9.3.4 Section 2(3) deals with the degree of care ordinarily expected from visitors

By s 2(3)(a) an occupier must be prepared for children to be less careful than adults.

Simkiss v Rhondda BC (1983)

The plaintiff, a girl of seven, fell down a bluff, ie a cliff with a perpendicular broad face, occupied by the defendant and opposite a block of flats where the plaintiff lived. Her father had not thought that his little girl would try to slide down that slope and the slope was only dangerous if somebody tried to do so.

Held (CA) that the defendants were not in breach of their duty under s 2 by failing to fence the bluff. If the defendants were required to fence off that ground it would be required to fence off every bluff which was near a housing estate. An occupier was entitled to assume that a prudent parent would act reasonably in warning his children of natural hazards.

Note

When a child is a trespasser, s 2(3)(a) will have *no* application and resort must be had to Occupiers Liability Act 1984 below.

By s 2(3)(b) an occupier may expect that a person, in the exercise of his calling, will appreciate and guard against any special risks ordinarily incident to it, so far as the occupier leaves him free to do so.

Field v Jeavons (1965)

An occupier of a factory was held liable to a servant of a contractor; a circular saw was resting on a bed; the plaintiff was an electrician who was making the electrical connection; a servant of the defendant negligently switched on with the result that the saw 'walked', injuring the plaintiff.

Held (CA) that the defendant was liable, subject to a finding of contributory negligence of 25%.

Salmon v Seafarer Restaurants (1983)

Held the liability to a *fireman* was not limited to liability for exceptional risk. Liability was based on ordinary principles, special skills of a fireman were only a factor to be taken into account; occupier was under the *ordinary* duty under s 2.

Held the defendant was liable to the plaintiff fireman as (1) fire was caused by employee's negligence; (2) injuries to the plaintiff were directly caused by that negligence; (3) the plaintiff's presence was reasonably foreseeable.

9.3.5 Section 2(4) provides that in determining whether the occupier of premises has discharged the common duty of care to a visitor, regard must be had to all the circumstances of the case

By s 2(4)(a) where damage is caused to a visitor by a danger of which he had been warned by the occupier, such a warning does not 'without more' – that is *by itself* – absolve the occupier unless in all the circumstances it was enough to enable the visitor to be reasonably safe.

Roles v Nathan (1963)

The subsection was considered in this case. The defendant was occupier of premises where there had been difficulty in lighting a boiler; the plaintiff chimney sweeps were twice warned about the danger of fumes and on the second occasion had to be forcibly dragged out; when they returned to complete the work they were overcome by carbon monoxide fumes and were found dead the next day.

Held (CA 2–1) that with this history of warnings the defendant was not liable. Pearson LJ dissented on the evidence, particularly by the fact that a servant of the defendant had relit the boiler before it should have been done.

Section 2(4)(b) provides that where damage is caused to a visitor by danger due to the fault of an *independent contractor* employed by the occupier, the occupier is not liable for that, by itself, provided he took such steps as were reasonable to satisfy himself that the contractor was competent and that the work had been properly done.

AMF v Magnet Bowling (1968)

The plaintiff was the owner of valuable timber to be used by them in lay-
ing a bowling alley belonging to D1; D2 was the independent contractor of
D1 and had contracted to build the alley. In due course the timber was
delivered and was in the process of being installed by the plaintiff. One
night there was a rain storm, the building became flooded and the timber
was ruined.

Held both DD were liable to the plaintiff, their visitor. There had been
insufficient precautions taken by D2 to guard against entry of flood water.
D1 could not rely on s 2(4)(b) as there had been no supervision by them of
D2 and no instructions had been given regarding anti-flooding precautions. Following *Wheat v Lacon* (1966) above, D2 was an occupier *as well as*
D1 and was liable under Occupiers' Liability Act for failure to take reasonable care with regard to temporary precautions against flooding.

Haseldine v Daw (1941)

This is an illustration of the operation of the subsection although a pre-
1957 case. Plaintiff visited a block of flats to see a tenant; the plaintiff used
a lift which was in the occupation of the defendant, owner of the flats; due
to the negligence of a firm of engineers employed by the defendant to
repair the lift, the plaintiff was injured when lift fell to the bottom of the
lift shaft.

Held (CA) that the defendants, having employed a competent firm of
engineers, had *discharged* the duty owed to the plaintiff. Defendant had no
technical knowledge and to have held him responsible for the fault of his
independent contractor would have been to make him an *insurer* of the
safety of his lift.

Ferguson v Welsh (1987)

The House of Lords here considered the position of the independent contractor. Plaintiff was employed by D1 to assist in the demolition of a building owned by local council, D3. D2 had obtained the work and in breach
of contract subcontracted the job to D1 who used an unsafe system of
work; the plaintiff fell and was severely injured. In breach of contract neither D1 or D2 had public liability insurance. Plaintiff sought to recover
damages, agreed at £150,000, against D3 on the basis of occupier's liability.

Held that an occupier would not normally be liable to an employee of a
contractor employed to carry out work on the occupier's premises if the
employee were injured as a result of an unsafe system of work used by *his*
employer, the contractor, since it would not be reasonable to expect the
occupier to supervise the contract to ensure that the contractor would
carry out the duty *he* owed to *his* employees to use a safe system of work.

Held that D2 possibly had ostensible authority from D3 to invite the plaintiff and D1 on to premises but the plaintiff's injury did not arise from any 'use'
of premises by him which gave rise to the common duty of care under s 2(2).

The House of Lords held then that the plaintiff's claim against D3 failed.

Per Lord Keith:

It would be going a very long way to hold that an occupier of premises is liable to the employee of an independent contractor engaged to do work on the premises in respect of damages arising, not from the physical state of the premises, but from an unsafe system of work adopted by the contractor.

9.3.6 Section 2(5) provides that the common duty of care does not impose on an occupier any obligation to a visitor in respect of risks willingly accepted as his by the visitor (the question whether a risk was so accepted to be decided on the same principles as in other cases in which one person owes a duty of care to another)

Thus the defence of *volenti non fit injuria* remains available to the occupier.

Simms v Leigh Rugby Club (1969)

The plaintiff was playing in a Rugby League football match; he broke his leg in the act of scoring a try when tackled by two opponents. Plaintiff alleged that the fracture was caused by being thrown against a concrete barrier 7ft 3 inches from the touch line.

Held that the accident had *not* happened in the way described by the plaintiff. But even if had, there was no breach of the common duty of care required by s 2(2). The barrier complied with the bylaws of the governing body of the game which provided that there should be a distance of 7ft from the touch line to the ringside. Section 2(5) was a defence as footballers who went to the defendant's ground went willingly accepting the risks that arose from playing the game under the rules of the League, on a ground approved by the League.

9.3.7 Section 2(6) provides for the purpose of this section that persons who enter premises for any purpose in the exercise of a right conferred by law are to be treated as permitted by the occupier to be there for that purpose whether they in fact have his permission or not

Greenhalgh v British Railways Board (1969)

The Court of Appeal held this subsection was for the purposes of s 2 which defines only the extent of the occupier's duty to *acknowledged* visitors. The subsection does not expand the range of persons who were to be treated as visitors. Facts were that the plaintiff was walking over a railway bridge, a *public* right of way, when she tripped over a pot-hole.

Held (CA) that the claim failed as she was not a visitor. At common law such a person had never been regarded as an invitee or licensee and thus could not be a visitor under the Act.

Holden v White (1982)

The plaintiff slipped when stepping on a defective manhole; he was using a *private* right of way across the defendant's land.

Held (CA) that he was not the defendant's visitor as he would not have been treated as an invitee or licensee of the defendant at common law.

See now Occupier's Liability Act 1984 below.

9.4 Damage to property

9.4.1 By s 1(3)(b) the Act applies to the obligations of a person occupying or having control of any premises or structures in respect of damage to property including the property of persons who are not themselves his visitors

9.4.2 Occupier has no duty to protect the goods of his visitor from the risk of theft by third parties

Tinsley v Dudley (1951)

The plaintiff went to a public house, not a common inn, and before entering he left his motor cycle in a yard which formed part of the premises. No charge was made for the use of the yard and no attendant was provided; the publican was not informed of the presence of the machine. When leaving the premises the plaintiff discovered that his motor cycle had been stolen.

Held (CA) that his claim against the publican failed.

Per Jenkins LJ:

There is no warrant at all on the authorities, so far as I know, for holding that an invitor, where the invitation extends to the goods as well as to the person of the invitee, thereby by implication of law assumes a liability to protect the invitee and his goods, not merely from physical dangers arising from defects in the premises, but from the risk of the goods being stolen by some party ... the defendant here can only be fixed with liability if the inference can properly be drawn from the circumstances that there was an actual or constructive delivery of the plaintiff's motor cycle into his safe keeping. On the facts it seems to me that clearly there was no such delivery, actual or constructive.

9.5 Restriction of liability

9.5.1 Section 2(1) provides for a duty of care to all visitors except in so far as occupier is free to, and does, modify or exclude his obligation by agreement or otherwise

Ashdown v Williams (1957)
The plaintiff was a licensee of the defendant; when crossing his land she was injured by railway trucks which were being negligently shunted; the defendant had posted a notice that all persons using the land were there at their own risk and would have no claim against the defendant.

Held (CA) that notice absolved the defendant from liability for negligence; the plaintiff had read first few lines of the notice and could have read the rest of the notice.

White v Blackmore (1972)
The deceased was a competitor at a 'jalopy' meeting; at the entrance and around the track there were warning notices absolving organisers from liability for accidents to spectators *howsoever* caused; deceased competed in one race and then watched another; a car collided with a safety rope which was then pulled out; then, because of negligent staking, the spectators' rope was also pulled out; as a result White was catapulted into the air and subsequently died from his injuries. The Court of Appeal was unanimous that *volenti non fit injuria* was no defence.

Held 2–1 that the defendants had effectively excluded their liability as they were entitled so to do under s 2(1); the deceased was a spectator and was subject to the condition set out in the warning notice.

9.5.2 The Unfair Contract Terms Act 1977
The Act applies to all attempts to exclude or limit business liability for negligence.

Section 1(3) defines business liability as arising from things done or to be done by a person in the course of a business or from the occupation of premises for the business purposes of the occupier.

Section 2(1) prevents the exclusion or restriction of liability by contractual term or by *notice* for *death* or *personal injury* resulting from *negligence*.

Section 2(2) provides that in the case of *other* loss or damage, liability for negligence can only be excluded or restricted when it is *reasonable*.

By Section 2(3) a person's agreement to or awareness of such a term or notice is not of itself to be taken as indicating his voluntary acceptance of any risk.

Q Would *Ashdown v Williams* and *White v Blackmore* be decided the same way today?

9.5.3 The Occupiers' Liability Act 1984

Section 1(1) provides that the duty is owed by an occupier 'to persons other than his visitors'. The Act therefore applies to persons using *private* rights of way and persons exercising rights under the National Parks Act 1949.

Holden v White is now overruled. Persons using a public right of way are unaffected.

By s 1(3) the duty is owed by an occupier to a 'trespasser' provided:

(a) he is *aware* of the danger or has *reasonable grounds* to believe that it exists;

(b) he *knows* or has *reasonable grounds* to believe that the other is or may be in the vicinity of danger;

(c) the risk is one which in all the circumstances of the case he may reasonably be expected to guard against.

Section 1(4) provides that the occupier owes a duty to take such care as is reasonable in all the circumstances of the case to see that the trespasser does not suffer injury on the premises by reason of the danger concerned.

By s 1(5) the duty owed may be discharged when *warning* of the danger is given.

By s 1(7) Act does not apply to persons exercising a *public* right of way. Thus *Greenhalgh v BRB* (1969) is unaffected.

By s 1(8) The Act does not cover damage to property.

Section 2 now excludes from the ambit of 'business liability' liabilities incurred in the course of persons visiting in the pursuit of recreational or educational purposes rather than the actual business of the occupier, providing the actual letting in of the public is not part of the business.

Thus a farmer may now exclude his liability to rock climbers.

9.6 Liability to trespassers

9.6.1 At common law an occupier must treat a trespasser with 'common humanity'

British Railways Board v Herrington (1972)

The plaintiff aged six was playing with other children on National Trust property; immediately adjoining the property was the defendant's electrified railway line; boundary was marked by a fence which was in a state of very bad repair; when the plaintiff strayed from his playmates he was able to get over it; he then came into contact with the 'live' rail and was severely injured. A well-trodden path showed that many trespassers must have crossed the line at this point to other National Trust property on the other side. Further, there was evidence that a few weeks before the accident some children had been seen on the line.

Held (HL) that there was a duty to treat a trespasser with common humanity. Where occupier knew of physical facts which involved danger of serious injury to an anticipated trespasser, his duty was to take reasonable steps to enable trespasser to avoid the danger. Because the relationship was forced on him, the occupier's duty to act in a humane manner was – unlike a duty of care – subjective; trespassers must take the occupier as they find him. On that test, the defendants were liable; they knew children played on the other side of the fence and they must have known that a young child might cross a defective fence and run into grave danger – yet they did nothing.

9.6.2 The Occupiers Liability Act (1984)
Gives statutory expression of the occupiers duty to trespassers – above.

Section 1(3) defines *when* a duty is owed and s 1(4) declares the content of that duty.

9.6.3 Liability of non-occupiers to trespassers
Occupier's liability to a trespasser is not necessarily the same as the liability of some other person who carries on an activity on the land.

Buckland v Guildford Gas (1948)
A girl aged 13 climbed an attractive tree and was electrocuted when she came into contact with the defendant's high voltage wires, which were hidden in the foliage at the top.

Held the defendants were held liable because they were in breach of their duty to take *reasonable* care for the safety of someone who might reasonably have been contemplated as likely to be affected by their lack of care – the wires were dangerously close to the tops of the trees. On the facts that girl's presence should have been foreseen.

9.7 Liability to children
An 'allurement', ie something fatal and fascinating, may tempt a child on to the land and make his presence foreseeable.

Glasgow Corporation v Taylor (1921)
A boy aged seven died from eating the berries of a poisonous shrub in a public garden owned by the defendant.

Held (HL) that the defendant was liable because they knew of the presence of children; berries were attractive to such a child as the plaintiff and the defendant had done nothing to fence off the shrub or to warn children of its dangers.

Pannet v McGuiness (1972)
The defendant demolition contractors were demolishing a warehouse near a public park; towards the end of the job hoardings were taken down and fires were lit to burn rubbish; men were employed to feed the fires and to

keep a look-out for children; soon after school hours the men went off, leaving site unattended. Plaintiff, aged five, went on site and fell into a fire; previously he had been chased off, but that was before fires were lit.

Held (CA) that the defendants *were* liable; it was not sufficient to chase off children; presence of children was likely, and there was the added attraction of fires. There had been a failure of common sense and humanity caused by the failure of the workmen.

Q Toytown Council acquires a house by compulsory purchase; it is left standing empty and children begin to play there. Dodger, a child aged eight, enters the house through a window; whilst playing in the house he falls down the stairs, injuring himself. Advise Dodger.

9.7.1 An occupier is entitled to assume that children of tender years will be accompanied by a responsible person

Phipps v Rochester Corporation (1955)
Two children went blackberrying, the plaintiff, a boy aged five, was accompanied by his sister aged seven; they walked across a field which was in the process of being developed as a housing estate; the boy fell into a trench and broke his leg.

Held that the defendants were not in breach of their duty to him as a licensee; they were entitled to assume that the children would be accompanied by a responsible person.

Per Devlin J:

> The responsibility for the safety of little children must rest primarily on the parents; it is their duty to see that such children are not allowed to wander about by themselves, or at least to satisfy themselves that the places to which they do allow their children to go unaccompanied are safe for them to go to. It would not be socially desirable if parents were, as a matter of course, able to shift the burden of looking after children from their own shoulders to those of persons who happen to have accessible bits of land.

O'Connor v BTC (1958)
Mother and a child aged three, were waiting, in a guard's van of an express train, to enter restaurant car; van had an internal handle especially designed for guards and thus unusually easy to open. While the mother stood with her back to the door, obtaining a light for her cigarette, her child opened the door, fell out and was killed. There was no defect in the handle or lock.

Held (CA) that the defendants had not failed in their duty of care; the defendants were required to make provision for the safety of children of tender years on the basis that they would be accompanied by someone capable of looking after them; it was not reasonable to allow a child under four, who had never been in a train before, to wander across the carriage to the door.

9.7.3 Test of humanity did not always assist a trespassing child

Penny v Northampton BC (1974)

A child played on the defendant's large rubbish tip; he was injured when another boy threw an aerosol can into a fire. It was impracticable to fence the whole of the tip.

Held (CA) that there was no breach of duty by the defendant despite the fact that the defendant knew children frequently trespassed there. Humane occupier would have considered it to be a waste of time to improve fencing of tip which had eight entrances.

9.8 Liability of non-occupiers

9.8.1 Contractors

Whoever actually creates a source of danger, even on premises not in his occupation, is bound to use reasonable care to see that lawful visitors are reasonably safe whilst there.

Billings v Riden (1958)

The House of Lords held that a contractor working on premises owed a duty to take reasonable care to prevent injury to persons whom he might reasonably expect to be affected by his work. A contractor had left access to a house in dangerous condition so that the plaintiff, an old lady who was a *licensee* (a pre-1957 case), was injured when trying to leave. Her claim against contractor succeeded; her knowledge did *not* amount to contributory negligence.

Rimmer v Liverpool Council (1984)

The plaintiff was tenant of the defendant's flat; through their architect's department the defendant had built, in 1959, the plaintiff's flat with a dangerous glass panel; the plaintiff fell and put his hand through the panel.

Held (CA) that the defendant, as their own architect and builder, owed their tenant a duty to take reasonable care in designing and constructing the flat to see that it was reasonably safe when they let it to him; they had failed in that duty.

Targett v Torfaen BC (1992)

The plaintiff was tenant of a council house which had been designed and built by the defendant council; access to the house was down two flights of stone steps; there was no handrail for the lower steps and no effective lighting; one night the plaintiff fell down steps and was injured; he claimed damages for his personal injury against the council.

Held (CA) that the landlord, who was responsible for the design and construction of the house let by him, was under a duty to take reasonable care that the house was free from defects likely to cause injury to any person whom he ought reasonably to have in contemplation as likely to be affected by such defect. On that test council owed the plaintiff a duty of care to provide a handrail or lighting for the steps. Plaintiff's knowledge of a defect in building did not, by itself negative the duty of care or break the chain of causation since it was not always possible for the plaintiff to take steps to avoid the danger. Action succeeded and the Court of Appeal assessed contributory negligence at 25%.

10 Trespass to the person

Trespass to the person occurs when the defendant inflicts direct physical harm on the plaintiff.

10.1 Plaintiff must allege either intention or negligence

Fowler v Lanning (1959)

The plaintiff was a member of a shooting party; someone shot him; in his Statement of Claim he alleged 'the defendant shot the plaintiff'. The defendant applied to have the statement of claim struck out as disclosing no cause of action.

Held (by the judge in chambers, Diplock J) that it should be struck out; the plaintiff had to allege either that the shooting was intentional or that it was negligent; if it were unintentional and not negligent, then there was no action at all. It was not enough simply to allege the direct act – the shooting.

Q Would it have assisted the plaintiff in Fowler if he had pleaded *res ipsa loquitur?*

10.2 The limitation period is the same, whether the action be pleaded in trespass or negligence

Letang v Cooper (1965)

The defendant ran over the plaintiff in his car whilst she was sunbathing; more than three years after the accident the plaintiff served a writ on the defendant for trespass to the person. By the Law Reform (Limitation of Actions) Act 1954 the limitation period for personal injuries was three years. Defendant claimed the plaintiff's action was statute barred. Trial judge held she was entitled to a six-year limitation period as she had brought her action in trespass not negligence.

Held (CA) first that the Act provided that actions for damages for personal injuries, for negligence, nuisance or breach of duty, the limitation period was three years. Held that the action in question was caught by the statute as any trespass involved a breach of duty. But the Court of Appeal went on to say that to be actionable the trespass had to be inflicted either intentionally or negligently. If it were intentional then it was a battery. If it were negligent then it was an action in negligence and so was caught by the statute when it spoke of an action in negligence. Lord Denning MR held that a 'negligent trespass' was no longer a separate tort but simply negligence. Diplock LJ preferred to use the term 'negligence' but did not object to 'negligent trespass'.

Per Diplock LJ:

> It is essential to realise that when, since 1873, the name of a form of action is used to identify a cause of action, it is used as a convenient and succinct description of a particular category of factual situation which entitles one person to obtain from the court a remedy against another person. To forget this will indeed encourage the old forms of action to rule us from their graves.

10.3 Assault is the tort of putting another in the fear – reasonable apprehension – of violence

Stephens v Myers (1830)

The plaintiff was chairman of a meeting; the defendant made many interruptions and it was agreed that he should be evicted; the defendant then advanced on the plaintiff, declaring he would pull him from the chair, but was stopped before he could reach him.

Held that this constituted an assault.

Q Bull points an unloaded gun at the head of Finch. Advise Finch.

10.4 Battery is the tort of directly applying force to a person, hostilely or against his will

Coward v Baddley (1859)

The plaintiff saw the defendant trying to extinguish a fire; the plaintiff thought water should be directed elsewhere and touched the defendant to draw his attention; the defendant gave him into the custody of a policeman.

Held this was unjustified as there had been no battery.

Donnelly v Jackman (1970)

A police constable tapped accused on shoulder to stop him so as to talk to him; the accused then retaliated by striking constable with some force.

Held this was not legitimate self-defence as there had been no initial battery.

Bentley v Brudzuski (1982)

Here the officer's attempt to prevent the accused from leaving amounted to more than a trivial interference with the accused's liberty and was an unlawful attempt to detain him; thus it followed that accused was entitled to use self-defence for the officer was acting outside the scope of his duty.

10.4.1   Physical contact may be generally acceptable

Collins v Willcock (1984)

A WPC took arm of the accused whom she suspected of soliciting for the purposes of prostitution; WPC intended to detain her to administer a caution; there was no arrest.

Held (CA) this action to be a battery; the accused then had not assaulted her, when scratching her, in execution of her duty.

Per Goff LJ:

The fact that the statute – Street Offences Act 1959 – recognises the practice of cautioning by providing a review procedure does not, in our judgment, carry with it an implication that police officers have the power to stop and detain women for the purpose of implementing the system of cautioning. If it had been intended to confer any such power on police officers that power could and should, in our judgment, have been expressly conferred by the statute ... Since the police woman had not been exercising her powers of arrest when she detained the appellant, and since taking her arm to detain her went beyond lawful physical contact between two citizens it followed that the officer's act constituted a battery on the appellant and that she had not been acting in the execution of her duty when the assault occurred.

Per Goff LJ:

Generally speaking, consent is a defence to battery; and most of the physical contacts of ordinary life are not actionable because they are impliedly consented to by all who move in society and so expose themselves to the risk of bodily contacts. So nobody can complain of the jostling which is inevitable from his presence in, for example, a supermarket, an underground station or a busy street; nor can a person who attends a party complain if his hand is seized in friendship, or even if his back is (within reason) slapped. Although such cases are regarded as examples of implied consent, it is more common nowadays to treat them as falling within a general exception embracing all physical contact which is generally acceptable in the ordinary conduct of daily life.

Q Witless accidentally drives his car over the feet of PC Plod. After an altercation Witless refuses to move the car to release PC Plod. Has any tort been committed and if so, by whom?

10.5 False imprisonment: the imposition of a total restraint for some period, however short, upon the liberty of another without lawful justification

10.5.1 It is a moot point whether it is essential that the plaintiff should be aware of the restraint

Herring v Boyle (1834)

A boy was kept at school during the holidays by the headmaster as a form of security for fees he was seeking to obtain from the boy's mother; the boy was unaware of the detention. Court of Exchequer held that there was no evidence of imprisonment.

Meering v Grahame White (1919)

Here, however, the Court of Appeal held 2–1 that knowledge was not essential. Facts were that the plaintiff was suspected of stealing and was asked to go to the company office for questioning; he was told his evidence was required but, unknown to him, two employees were posted outside the room; when the police arrived he was arrested for theft; later he was tried and acquitted.

Held he was entitled to succeed in his action for false imprisonment against his employers, for he would not have been allowed to leave had he attempted to do so. Atkin LJ thought that a man could be imprisoned whilst asleep, drunk or insane even though, when returning to his senses, he was free to go.

Murray v Ministry of Defence (1988)

Meering was approved and Herring doubted. Facts were that the plaintiff was suspected of having committed offences involving the collection of money for the IRA, a prohibited organisation. Acting on orders, the defendant and five other soldiers went to the plaintiff's house at 7 am to arrest the plaintiff. Defendant remained with the plaintiff whilst soldiers assembled other occupants in one room and searched the house. At 7.30 am the defendant formally arrested the plaintiff.

Held (HL) that where a person was detained or restrained by a police officer and knew he was so detained or restrained, that amounted to an arrest even though no formal words of arrest were spoken by the officer. Thus the plaintiff was under arrest from 7 am to 7.30 am. Circumstances of the plaintiff's arrest were such that it was reasonable for the defendant to delay speaking the words of arrest until the plaintiff and soldiers were leaving the house, although in ordinary circumstances police should tell a person the reason for his arrest at the time when the arrest is made. Appeal by the plaintiff dismissed.

Per Lord Griffiths:

If a person is unaware that he has been falsely imprisoned and has suffered no harm, he can normally recover no more than nominal damages, and it is tempting to redefine the tort in the terms of the present rule in the American Law Institute's Restatement of the Law of Tort [which requires that the person confined 'is conscious of the confinement or is harmed by it']. On reflection however, I would not do so. The law attaches supreme importance to the liberty of the individual and if he suffers a wrongful interference with that liberty it should remain actionable even without proof of special damage.

10.5.2 It is not necessary that there should be any physical contact

Warner v Riddiford (1858)
The plaintiff had been taken into custody in his own house by the defendant and two police officers; he had submitted to their control and could not leave the room without their permission and attendance.
Held this to be imprisonment.

10.5.3 There are no degrees of imprisonment

Hague v Deputy Governor of Parkhurst Prison (1991)
A prisoner made a claim for false imprisonment; he alleged that he had been falsely imprisoned and unlawfully assaulted and battered by certain police officers when placed in a punishment block and stripped.
Held (HL) that his claim for false imprisonment should be struck out. While in prison he had no liberty to be in any place other than where the prison regime required him to be and therefore he had no liberty capable of deprivation by the prison regime, which could constitute the tort of false imprisonment.
Per Lord Bridge:

The concept of the prisoner's 'residual liberty' as a species of freedom of movement within the prison, enjoyed as a legal right which the prison authorities cannot lawfully restrain, seems to me quite illusory.

Per Lord Jauncey:

Imprisonment is either lawful or false and questions of degree dependent on whether or not the breach is substantial do not arise, since the definition of the tort of false imprisonment is total deprivation.

The House of Lords was prepared to hold that a prisoner who was subjected to intolerable conditions of detention, seriously prejudicial to his health, had the public law remedy of judicial review and if he sustained injury to health, an action in negligence.

10.5.4   It matters not how short the duration of the imprisonment

Mee v Cruikshank (1902)
A prisoner had been acquitted and was then taken down to the cells for brief questioning by prison officers.

Held to have been falsely imprisoned, he should have been released from the very moment of acquittal.

10.5.5   There must be a total restraint

Bird v Jones (1845)
In this case there was a regatta on the Thames; a footpath on Hammersmith bridge was wrongfully fenced off to provide seating for spectators. Plaintiff wished to assert his right to use the footpath and climbed the barrier; he was stopped by the police from so proceeding and remained there for half an hour; all that time he was free to go back or cross using the carriageway.

Held there was no false imprisonment as there was no total restraint.

10.5.6   Plaintiff is not restrained if he has consented to the confinement

Herd v Weardale Steel Co Ltd (1915)
A miner was taken down to a coal face; in breach of recognised procedure he refused to work, alleging unsafe working conditions; he requested to be raised immediately to the surface but was made to wait 20 minutes before being taken up.

Held (HL) that the plaintiff was responsible for his own predicament for he had chosen to go down the mine on certain conditions – *volenti non fit injuria*.

10.5.7   Entry and exit to premises may be subject to conditions

Robinson v Balmain Ferry (1910)
In this case there was a pier and by the regulations a penny was to be paid by those who entered and a further penny to be paid on exit. Plaintiff paid his penny to enter with the intention of boarding a ferry for which there would be no further charge; he changed his mind and tried to leave without paying his penny at the exit turnstile. Defendant refused to let him leave until he had paid.

Held (JCPC) that this was not false imprisonment, there was no duty to make exit free to those who had come by definite contract involving their leaving by another way and a charge of a penny was reasonable; notice of the conditions was immaterial.

Q Reckless boards a train and the guard locks the carriage door; later the train stops at a signal and Reckless wishes to alight, to take a short cut home. The guard refuses to unlock the door. Advise Reckless.

10.6 Justification of trespass to the person

10.6.1 Defence of person or property

It is justifiable to use force to remove a trespasser but force used must not be excessive.

Collins v Rennison (1754)

The defendant pleaded that he had found the plaintiff upon a ladder in the defendant's garden, nailing a board to the defendant's wall; he requested the plaintiff to come down and on his refusing, gently shook the ladder and gently threw the plaintiff to the ground.

Held plea was bad as force used was excessive; in any case it did not and could not prevent the trespass.

Kenlin v Gardner (1966)

Police officers caught hold of the accused in order to question him; he had not realised who they were and tried to run away, striking them.

Held (by a Divisional court) that as the police were not arresting him their action was a technical battery; accused was then permitted to use reasonable force in self defence, with the result the his conviction for assaulting police in the execution of their duty was quashed.

See also *Collins v Wilcock* (1984) above.

10.6.2 Parental and other authority

R v Newport (Salop) Justices (1929)

Boys were caned for smoking in the street after school hours.

Held punishment was reasonable and no battery.

10.6.3 Judicial Authority

The interposition of a judicial authority will be a bar to a claim for false imprisonment.

Austin v Dowling (1870)

The defendant's wife arrested the plaintiff and gave him into custody; the defendant signed charge sheet after being warned by a police inspector that the inspector would not incur any responsibility.

Held that after such a warning, signing the charge sheet was the act which caused the imprisonment; the inspector had acted ministerially, not judicially. Defendant then was responsible for the imprisonment.

Meering v Grahame-White (1919)

In this case, however, the Court of Appeal, although deeming the defendants to be liable for false imprisonment, awarded nominal damages only; this was recompense for the hour that the plaintiff had spent in the waiting room; the subsequent detention was caused by the judicial act of the police officers in arresting the plaintiff.

Note ────────────────────────────────────

The factual situation in *Austin* was unusual and *Meering* represents the usual state of affairs.

Davidson v Chief Constable of North Wales (1994)

H, a friend of the plaintiff, purchased a cassette at a store and then returned to the cassette counter to talk to plaintiff. They stood there talking before leaving the store. Store detective believed that they had left without paying for the cassette; she rang the police and on their arrival told them of her suspicion and pointed out the suspects. Police arrested plaintiff and H on suspicion of shop-lifting; H denied dishonesty, produced the cassette but had lost receipt; plaintiff remained silent. They were taken to the police station but were released after two hours when police received a phone message from a shop assistant, confirming that H had paid for the cassette. Police officers at trial gave evidence that they had acted independently, exercising their own judgment in arresting plaintiff and H.

Held (CA) police officers had been justified in arresting plaintiff and H because they had a reasonable suspicion, derived from information supplied by the store detective, that they had been shop-lifting. *Police and Criminal Evidence Act 1984* s 24(6) was a complete defence.

Second, on the facts, store detective had merely given information to a proper authority; there was no evidence that she had gone beyond that. Trial judge had been right to withdraw the case from the jury.

Per Sir Thomas Bingham MR:

The essential test that is applied is ... whether the defendant gave the information to a prosecuting authority so that what followed was the result of that prosecuting authority or whether the defendants themselves were responsible for the acts that followed ... what Mrs Yates did and said in no way went beyond the mere giving of information, leaving it to the officers to exercise a discretion which on their own unchallenged evidence they did as to whether they should take action or no.

Meering v Grahame-White applied.

10.6.4 Powers of arrest

At common law any person has the power to arrest where there is a breach of the peace

Albert v Lavin (1981)

The accused caused a disturbance at a bus queue and was arrested by a police officer in plain clothes; the officer was then assaulted by the accused.

Held (HL) that it did not matter that the accused was unaware that his arrester was a policeman. Every citizen, in whose presence a breach of the peace is being, or reasonably appears to be about to be, committed, has the right and duty to take steps to prevent the breach. The only difference between a citizen and a constable is that the duty of the citizen is one of imperfect obligation, ie it cannot be enforced.

For a lawful arrest by a private person, the arrestable offence must have been committed by someone

Walters v WH Smith (1914)

The plaintiff had been arrested by a private person for theft; a marked copy of a book, taken from the defendant's book stall, had been found on the plaintiff's book stall. He was employed by the defendant but in defiance of company's rules, ran his own business. At his trial he was acquitted.

Held he succeeded in his action for false imprisonment; his arrest had not been lawful for no offence had been committed.

John Lewis Ltd v Tims (1952)

Mother and her daughter were arrested for shoplifting; daughter was convicted but case against mother was withdrawn.

Held (HL) that the arrest of the mother was lawful – the suspicion was reasonable and the offence had been committed.

When arrested by a private person, the arrested person must be taken before a magistrate or a police officer as soon as is reasonably possible

John Lewis v Tims (1952)

The plaintiff and her daughter were under observation by store detectives who saw daughter take goods and place them in her mother's bag; they were arrested and taken to the managing director's office; this was a routine step so as to give them a further opportunity for explanation and also to exercise control over the store detectives. The daughter at her trial was convicted but case against the plaintiff was withdrawn.

Held (HL) that her claim for false imprisonment failed. As the arrest was lawful, the delay in handing her over was the only cause of action; the delay in handing her over to the police was a short one, was reasonable and was in fact to her benefit.

Arrest by a constable

When arrested by a constable a longer delay is permissible for it is reasonable for a *constable* to investigate the circumstances of the case before taking the arrested person to a police station or before a magistrate.

Dallison v Caffery (1964)

The plaintiff sued police officer for false imprisonment and malicious prosecution; on his arrest the plaintiff protested his innocence and before being taken to the police station to be charged, the defendant, who was in charge of the case, took the plaintiff to his house and, with the defendant's permission, searched it; then the plaintiff was taken to his place of work to check the plaintiff's alibi; then the plaintiff was taken to police station and charged. At his trial prosecution offered no evidence and said a mistake had been made.

Held (CA) first, that the onus was on the defendant to prove reasonable cause and it was for the judge to decide it; on the facts, matter had rightly been decided in the defendant's favour. Secondly it was reasonable for a constable to investigate the circumstances of the case, eg to check on an alibi – before taking the arrested person to the police station or magistrate; thus in that case, there had been no false imprisonment for the period between arrest and the return to the police station.

The arrested person has the right to be informed at the time of arrest what is the act for which he is arrested

Christie v Leachinsky (1947)

The House of Lords *held* the plaintiff's claim succeeded because he had not been told, at the time of the arrest, of the true ground for it. However it was further held that the arrested person need not be so informed if it were quite obvious from the circumstances why he was being arrested, nor if his own conduct made it impossible to inform him.

10.7 The Police and Criminal Evidence Act 1984

By s 24(4) anyone may arrest without warrant anyone who is in the act of committing an arrestable offence or anyone whom he has reasonable grounds for suspecting to be committing such an offence.

By s 24(5) where an arrestable offence has been committed, any person may arrest without warrant anyone who is guilty of the offence or anyone whom he has reasonable grounds for suspecting to be guilty of it.

By s 24(6) a police officer may arrest without warrant anyone whom he suspects on reasonable grounds to have committed an arrestable offence even though the offence has not in fact been committed.

By s 24(7) a police officer may arrest without warrant anyone who is or whom he has reasonable grounds for suspecting to be about to commit an arrestable offence.

The distinction between police officers and private persons – demonstrated in *Walters v Smith* – has thus been unfortunately preserved.

Section 28 preserves the effect of *Christie v Leachinsky*.

Section 30 preserves *Dallison v Caffery*.

10.8 Intentional physical harm other than trespass to the person

An act wilfully done which is calculated to cause, and actually does cause, physical harm to another person, is a tort.

Wilkinson v Downton (1897)

The plaintiff was told by the defendant, as a joke, that her husband had been in an accident and had broken both his legs.

Held that he was liable to her for her nervous shock. An action in deceit lay for her railway fare.

Janvier v Sweeney (1919)

A woman servant was falsely told by a private detective that, unless she handed over private letters of her mistress, she would be given up to the authorities for corresponding with a German spy.

Held (CA) that she should recover damages for the resultant nervous shock.

Q Miss Alliance is very upset by a series of silent telephone calls. She suspects the identity of the caller. Has she any cause of action?

11 Breach of statutory duty

11.1 When breach of statutory duty is a tort

Plaintiff must show *causal connection* between the breach and the subsequent damage – *McWilliams v Sir William Arroll Ltd* (1962). See Chapter 3.

11.2 Plaintiff must show that the statute not only imposed a duty on the defendant but also gave a corresponding right to the plaintiff

11.2.1 Consideration must be given to the whole of the Act

Keating v Elvan (1968)

The plaintiff fell into a trench dug in a street by D1 as agent for D2, a local authority; a protective barrier had been removed by a stranger. D2 was sued for breach of statutory duty under Public Utilities Street Works Act 1950 s 8 'to secure that so long as the street is broken up it is adequately fenced and guarded'.

Held (CA) that s 8 – a small part of the Act – was concerned with providing protection for certain authorities, not for the protection of individuals who might suffer injury as a result of the defective state of a street.

11.2.2 If no penalty for its breach is imposed, it can be assumed that a civil right of action accrues to the person suffering loss by the breach

Reffell v Surrey CC (1964)

The plaintiff was injured as a result of defendant's breach of School Building Regulations which imposed no sanction.

Held she had a right of action for the breach

Thornton v Kirklees MBC (1979)

The plaintiff, a homeless person, sought damages from defendant on the basis that defendants, as a housing authority, were in breach of a statutory duty which they owed him under Housing (Homeless Persons) Act 1977 s 3. There was no provision for penalties against the local authority for any failure to carry out its statutory duty.

Held (CA) that the plaintiff could bring an action for damages and the action should proceed to trial.

11.2.3 Where a penalty for breach is imposed

The court may assume *prima facie* that there was no intention to confer, in addition, a right of action in tort.

Phillips v Britannia Hygienic Model Laundry (1923)

The defendant was sued by plaintiff for an accident caused by a wheel falling off one of the defendant's lorries; defendant had just had the lorry repaired by a reputable repairer; defendant was in breach of statutory duty despite the lack of personal negligence on defendant's part.

Held (CA) that the statutory duty concerning the safety of road vehicles was not enforceable by individuals injured by its breach; this was a public duty, the sole remedy for which was that provided by the statute itself – a £10 fine. Plaintiff's remedy at common law remained.

Coote v Stone (1971)

The plaintiff's car collided with defendant's car which was illegally parked in defiance of a Prohibition Order made under the Road Traffic Act 1960.

Held (CA) that the purpose of the Order was to facilitate the flow of traffic, *not* to give a member of the public a right to claim damages; a £20 fine was the *only* remedy for the breach.

Monk v Warbey (1935)

The defendant had permitted his car to be driven by X with the result that defendant was guilty of the statutory offence of permitting his car to be driven by an uninsured driver. Defendant was then liable to a criminal penalty. Plaintiff had been injured as a result of X's negligent driving.

Held (CA) that plaintiff *did* have an action against defendant.

Q Consider how *Monk v Warby* can be reconciled with *Phillips v Britannia*.

11.2.4 Where the statute imposes a duty for the protection of the plaintiff or a class of persons of whom he is one, it *prima facie* creates a correlative right vested in the plaintiff

Groves v Wimborne (1898)

The defendant manufacturer was held liable in damages to one of his servants; plaintiff had been injured as a result of defendant's failure to perform his statutory duty of fencing dangerous machinery. Since the Act was clearly passed in favour of workers and to compel employers to perform certain duties for their protection, plaintiff had a right of action *despite* the imposition of a special penalty; it mattered not that some or all of that penalty might be applied to plaintiff's benefit.

11.2.5 Plaintiff must be a member of the class for whose benefit the Act was passed

Cutler v Wandsworth Stadium (1949)

The defendants were under a statutory duty to provide space for book-makers at their greyhound race track; plaintiff was a bookmaker who had been unable to find such a space; he sued for breach of statutory duty.

Held (HL) that the claim failed as the Act was intended to regulate the conduct of betting for the benefit of *punters, not* for the benefit of book-makers; obligation was enforceable by criminal proceedings only.

Lonrho v Shell (1981)

The plaintiff claimed that defendants were in breach of a sanctions order directed against Southern Rhodesia and that as a result, UDI was pro-longed and so was the period when plaintiff's pipe line was disused.

Held (HL) that there was *no* cause of action; purpose of the sanctions was to stop delivery of oil to Southern Rhodesia, not to protect a particu-lar class of persons, such as the plaintiff, who were engaged in supplying oil to that country.

11.2.6 When an obligation has been imposed upon the undertakers of public utilities there is a presumption that a private interest shall be protected only by special remedy

Atkinson v Newcastle Waterworks (1877)

The defendant was in breach of its statutory duty to maintain a certain water pressure for the purpose of extinguishing fire – a penalty of £10 being paid for its breach. Plaintiff's home was damaged by fire as a direct result of defendant's failure to perform its duty.

Held (CA) that the intention of the legislature was that the penalty should be the *sole* remedy, otherwise defendant would virtually be the fire insurers of Newcastle.

11.2.7 Plaintiff's injury must come within the 'mischief' of the Act

Gorris v Scott (1874)

The plaintiff sued defendant ship owner for the loss of sheep which had been swept overboard in consequence of defendant's failure to supply pens and footholds as required by Contagious Diseases Act 1869.

Held plaintiff could not recover as the *purpose* of the statute was to pre-vent the spread of contagious disease – *not* to prevent animals from being washed overboard.

11.2.8 Statute may impose a duty to prevent injury in a particular manner

Nicholls v Austin (1946)

The plaintiff worker was injured by a piece of material flying out of machine on which she was working.

Held (HL) that the claim failed, for the duty to fence securely – Factory Act 1937 s 14 – was to prevent the *worker* from coming into contact with the machine.

Per Lord Simonds:

> The fence was intended to keep the worker out, not to keep the machine or its product in.

Donaghey v Boulton and Paul (1967)

The plaintiff fell through aperture of roof whilst moving asbestos sheets. Building Regulations 1948 required suitable support where work was being done on roofs covered with fragile material; crawling boards were not supplied.

Held (HL) that the breach caused the accident and plaintiff's claim succeeded even though plaintiff fell through the aperture and *not* through fragile material.

Per Lord Guest:

> The precise way in which the accident happened is not material if the accident which happened was the *type* of accident against which the regulation was designed.

11.2.9 Breach of statutory duty can form the foundation of a common law action

Manchester Corporation v Markland (1936)

A burst water main went unheeded for three days; there was a frost, ice formed and a car skidded, killing plaintiff. Corporation was statutory water authority and was not informed of the burst until after the accident.

Held (HL) that the driver of the car was properly exonerated but that the Corporation was liable in *negligence* for not having taken prompt steps to attend to the leak and in failing to take reasonable steps to inform themselves of leaks.

11.3 Whether a private right of action arises from a breach of statute is a matter of legislative intention

Hague v Deputy Governor of Parkhurst Prison (1991)

Hague was regarded as a trouble-maker and was ordered by the Deputy Governor to be transferred to Wormwood Scrubs and to be held there in segregation for 28 days. The order was in purported pursuance of R43 of the Prison Rules 1964. Hague challenged the legality of his segregation.

Held (HL) that his claim was for breach of statutory duty. The *fundamental question* was 'Did the legislature intend to confer on the plaintiff a cause of action for breach of statutory duty?' Rule 43 was not intended to confer a right of action on an individual prisoner. The rule was a purely preventative measure. Where the rule had been exercised in good faith it was inconceivable that the legislature intended to confer any cause of action on the segregated prisoner.

Hague's appeal was dismissed.

M (a minor) v Newham London BC (1994)

Child was suspected to have been sexually abused; she was interviewed by a psychiatrist and a social worker in the absence of her mother. Child, aged four, named abuser by his first name; interviewers both wrongly assumed that this was the mother's boyfriend who had the same name; in fact child was referring to a cousin. It was decided to move child from mother's care and local authority was granted care and control. The child was separated from her mother for almost a year. When mother saw a transcript of the interview she realised that child had not identified boyfriend as abuser and that there was no evidence to support that conclusion. Local authority accepted that fact and took steps to rehabilitate child with mother. Child and mother claimed defendants were in breach of their duty under the *Child Care Act 1980* to safeguard the welfare of children and claimed they suffered anxiety neurosis as a result of enforced separation. The Statement of Claim had been struck out as disclosing no reasonable cause of action.

Held (CA) that statutory duties imposed on local authority in relation to welfare of children were so general and unspecific that it was to be inferred that parliament did not intend that there should be a private law remedy for a breach of a local authority's duties under the Act.

Further held (2–1) that there was no duty of care at common law regarding the child, and held unanimously no duty of care to the mother. In the absence of an established category of negligence imposing on local authorities a duty of care in respect of a decision taken in the exercise of their statutory functions, it would not be fair or just – applying the incremental approach to the development of the law of negligence – to impose such a duty on the local authority.

Per Staughton LJ:

> I do not consider that the child was, in law and for all purposes, the patient of the psychiatrist in the Newham case. No doubt the medical profession would regard the child as the patient for some purposes, such as the duty of confidentiality. But the child had not sought the psychiatrist's services, nor had her mother as the person with parental responsibility on her behalf; those services

had been thrust upon them. The child was no more the patient than an applicant for life insurance who is examined by the company's doctor, or the errant motorist who is deprived of a small quantity of blood by the police surgeon. In all those cases the medical person without doubt owes *some* duty to the person being examined or treated. We have been asking the wrong question, whether any duty is owed. The right question is, *what* duty? It is a duty to use reasonable skill and care so as not to cause harm in the course of examination or treatment. But the general duty to perform the task allocated with reasonable skill and care – whether it be 'diagnosing' the name of an abuser, or assessing the expectation of life, or producing a blood sample for analysis – is in my opinion owed to the person who engages the doctor to perform that task. That is the health authority or the local council in the first case, the insurance company in the second, and the police authority in the third.

T (a minor) v Surrey CC (1994)

A mother saw an advertisement by Mrs W for child-minding; she contacted local authority's nursery and child-minding adviser, B, who confirmed that Mrs W was registered as a child-minder under the *Nurseries and Child-Minders Regulation Act 1948*; he told her there was no reason why T, her baby, could not safely be left in Mrs W's care. In fact less that three months earlier another child had been seriously injured, probably through violent shaking. Two case conferences at which B was present were unable to resolve whether Mrs W had caused the injury. she was not deregistered. Shortly after T's mother placed him with Mrs W, he suffered a serious injury similar to the injury suffered by the previous child.

Held claim for breach of statutory duty failed as failure by local authority to meet its implied obligations under the Act did not confer a private right of action. *Hague v Deputy Governor Parkhurst Prison* applied.

Second, there was no duty of care at common law based on failure to cancel registration of Mrs W.

Third, local authority *was* liable for a negligent misstatement – *Hedley-Byrne v Heller* applied.

Per Scott-Baker J:

If B had merely told Miss D that Mrs W was registered as a child-minder that would not, I think, have given rise to any liability. It would have been an accurate statement; but he went a good deal further. He told her he knew of no reason why T should not go to Mrs W, or words to that effect. There was, however, a very good reason why T should not go to Mrs W. another child had recently suffered a serious and unexplained injury whilst in her care.

11.4 Absolute statutory duties

11.4.1 A statutory duty may be absolute and so cannot be delegated; but if it is the plaintiff himself who is in default then defendant's liability may be diminished or extinguished

Ginty v Belmont (1959)

The plaintiff was working on a roof which he *knew* to be defective; he *knew* he was not to work on it without boards and he *knew* there were statutory regulations on the subject. Defendant provided him with boards which he failed to use and he fell through the roof, seriously injuring himself. There was an obligation on defendant, under Building Regulations 1948, to provide *and use* boards for that work.

Held the breach of defendant's duty consisted *of* and was co-extensive *with* the wrongful acts of the plaintiff and he therefore recovered *nothing*.

Per Pearson J:

> Has there been some fault on the part of the employer which goes beyond or is independent of the fault of the employee which, as a result of the doctrine of vicarious liability, constitutes a breach of statutory duty by the employer? In short, the fundamental question is: Whose fault was it?

Ross v Associated Portland Cement (1964)

The defendant employers had failed to provide the correct equipment and with some hesitation plaintiff's husband – a charge hand steel erector – decided to proceed without it. In so doing there was a breach of defendant's statutory duty to provide and maintain safe means of access to every working place. Defendant argued that they were not at all to blame because they were entitled to leave it to Ross to decide what to do; thus the sole cause of the accident was his well intentioned but mistaken decision to proceed.

Held (HL) that the failure of the employer to take any steps to see that proper equipment was available, contributed *a great deal* to the accident and *two-thirds* of the responsibility was apportioned to the employers.

Richardson v Stephenson Clarke Ltd (1969)

Here it was held, however, that the selection of equipment *was* properly left to the plaintiff, a competent and experienced man.

11.5 Defences

11.5.1 *Volenti non fit injuria* is no defence to a breach of statutory duty

Wheeler v New Merton Board Mills (1933)
The Court of Appeal held that it was no defence to a breach of statutory duty that workmen had consented to work on unguarded dangerous machinery. The reason for the rule is clear – if *volenti* were a defence, the intention of the legislative would be set at naught.

11.5.2 *Volenti* may be a defence where an employer is not in breach of any of his statutory duties

ICI v Shatwell (1964)
Two employees jointly decided to disregard safety measures in the face of express prohibition by both employer and statutory regulations.

Held (HL) that an employer *is* entitled to plead *volenti* to an action against him by *one* servant based on his vicarious responsibility for the conduct of the *other*, where the employer is *not* himself at fault.

Per Lord Reid:

> If the plaintiff invited or freely aided and abetted his fellow servant's disobedience then he is *volens* in the fullest sense. He cannot complain of the resulting injury either against the fellow servant or against the master on the grounds of his vicarious liability.

11.5.3 Contributory negligence may be pleaded

Uddin v Associated Portland Cement (1965)
A workman lost his arm when it was caught by unfenced dangerous machinery; he was trying to catch a pigeon in part of the factory where he had no authority to go.

Held (CA) he still recovered damages for breach of an absolute statutory duty though the damages were reduced by 80% because of his contributory negligence.

Per Diplock LJ:

> I do not think that the expression 'a frolic on his own' which is relevant for the purpose of making a master vicariously liable *for* the torts of his servant has any relevancy to the question of whether a master is liable *to* his servant either for breach of statutory duty or at common law – *Allen v Aeroplane and Motor Aluminium* (1965).

12 Employers' liability

The employer owes, at common law, a duty of care towards his servant.

12.1 There are three aspects of a master's duty

Wilson and Clyde Coal v English (1938)

The House of Lords held that master's duty was 'three fold – the provision of a competent staff of men, adequate material and a proper system and effective supervision' *per* Lord Wright.

12.2 Competent staff

Hudson v Ridge (1957)

A master was held liable for employing a man, who for four years, had had an incurable habit of tripping people.

O'Reilly v National Railway and Trainway Appliances (1966)

The plaintiff was employed by the defendant who bought scrap metal; in one load of scrap there was a live shell; the plaintiff was taunted by another employee X: 'Hit it! What are you afraid of?' Plaintiff did hit it and was seriously injured in the resultant explosion. He sued his employer on the grounds that they had failed to provide a safe place of work.

Held they were not liable; X's behaviour was one isolated act of misdemeanour for which they were not *personally* responsible; nor were they *vicariously* responsible as it was outside the scope of X's employment with them. X *himself* was responsible on the principle of *Donoghue v Stevenson*.

12.3 Adequate plant

Taylor v Rover Co Ltd (1966)

The plaintiff, who was employed by the defendant, lost an eye when a steel splinter flew from a defectively hardened chisel; the defendant *knew* – through the knowledge of a leading hand – that the same chisel had already caused an accident.

Held employer was liable because of this knowledge.

However, by Employer's Liability (Defective Equipment) Act 1969 s 1 where an employee suffers personal injury in the course of his employment in consequence of a defect in equipment provided by his employer, and the defect is attributable to the fault of a third party, the injury is *deemed* to be also attributable to negligence on the part of the employer.

Thus in *Taylor* the plaintiff would not now have to show personal fault on the part of the defendant – he is now *deemed* to be at fault.

12.4 Safe system

General Cleaning Contractors Ltd v Christmas (1952)

The plaintiff, a window cleaner, was instructed by the defendants to use 'sill' method, ie to stand on sill holding on to a sash while cleaning outside of windows; while using this method, the plaintiff's fingers were trapped inside lower sash suddenly closing and so causing him to fall.

Held (HL) that the defendants were liable because they had failed to instruct the plaintiff to test sashes for looseness before starting work; they had failed to provide wedges which, if inserted below lower sash, would have made the accident impossible. They had failed then to provide a safe system of work.

Thompson v Smiths Ship Repairers (1984)

The plaintiff recovered damages under master's common law duty in regard to *deafness* induced by exposure to loud noise over a long period. The general practice in heavy industry had been to ignore the risk of deafness but in 1963 Ministry of Labour had issued a pamphlet on industrial noise and thereafter expert advice and protective devices were available to employers; a prudent employer *would* have taken precautions after 1963. Damage to the plaintiff's hearing before 1963 could not be compensated for but the plaintiff was entitled to damages for as much of his hearing loss as could be attributed to the post-1963 exposure to excessive noise.

12.5 There is a duty to see that a safe system is enforced

Clifford v Challen (1951)

An employer was held liable for the failure to provide a safe system of work because he did not insist on the use of barrier cream; the cream was available but could only be obtained on demand; the foreman was not 'a great believer in it'. Plaintiff's damages were, however, reduced by 50% on the grounds of his contributory negligence.

12.6   Employer's duty is personal and non-delegable

McDermid v Nash Dredging Ltd (1987)

The plaintiff, a young and inexperienced deck hand, was working at the time of the accident on the deck of a tug in connection with dredging; the plaintiff's duty at the time was to tie and untie ropes; tug master went astern too quickly with the result that a rope snaked round the plaintiff's leg and pulled him into the water causing injuries which resulted in amputation. Plaintiff alleged a non-delegable duty resting on his employers to take reasonable care to provide a safe system of work.

Held (HL) that 'non-delegable' did not mean that the duty could not be delegated in the sense that it was incapable of being subject to delegation, but only that the employer could not escape responsibility if the duty had been delegated and was then not properly performed.

Held that the defendants had delegated *both* their duty of devising a safe system of work *and* its operation to the tug master who was negligent in failing to operate that system. Defendant liable then to the plaintiff.

12.7   A safe system may be enforced even when accident occurs abroad

Johnson v Coventry Churchill International Ltd (1992)

The plaintiff was an experienced joiner who was recruited by the English defendant to work in West Germany. Plaintiff travelled to Stuttgart and was directed to work on site being developed by a client of the defendant. Two weeks later the plaintiff suffered personal injuries whilst walking across two wooden planks positioned over an 8ft deep trench; one of the planks was rotten and gave way under his weight. West German law did not provide for an employer to be liable for personal injuries suffered by an employee as a result of employer's negligence.

Held the defendants were employing the plaintiff under a contract of service and had been under a duty of care to provide a safe system of work, including a safe means of access to the place of work; they were in breach of that duty.

Plaintiff *was* entitled to bring his action in England even though the wrong was *not* actionable in West Germany. *Rule* was that a wrong alleged to have been committed abroad was actionable in England as a tort *only* if it were an act which was actionable as a tort under English law *and* if it were actionable according to the law of the country where it was committed. Plaintiff failed the second leg of that test. However, there was an *exception* where it was a tort in England and *justice to the plaintiff* dictated that English law should be applied as England was the country, the law of which had the most significant relationship with the occurrence and the parties.

The application of English law to the issue would afford protection to

English workmen required to work abroad for English companies in countries of whose systems of law they could be expected to have little knowledge.

12.8 Unitary nature of duty

Wilson v Tyneside Window Cleaning Co (1958)

The plaintiff was a window cleaner of 56 with a lifelong experience of the trade; he was sent out by his employer to clean the windows of a brewery; whilst there he pulled on a window handle which came away; he fell and was injured. His only instruction from his employers, with whom he had been for 14 years, was that if he found a window which presented unusual difficulty or risk, he was to report to the defendant for further instructions.

Held (CA) that in the case of so experienced a workman as the plaintiff, the defendants had fulfilled their duty of care to take reasonable care for his safety, a duty which although often subdivided for purposes of argument, was one and the same.

Per Pearce LJ:

All three are ultimately only manifestations of the duty of the master to take reasonable care.

12.9 Strictness of the duty

12.9.1 Employer's duty is a duty of care only

Withers v Perry Chain Co (1961)

The Court of Appeal held that where an employee, with a previous history of dermatitis, was given the driest work possible, but still contacted dermatitis, this was not negligence on the defendant's part; they had done everything they reasonably could to protect the plaintiff, short of refusing to employ her at all; it could not be said that an employer was bound to dismiss an employee rather than allow her to run a small risk.

Jones v Lionite (1961)

The deceased was addicted to fumes from a degreasing solvent; foreman had warned him concerning this.

Held (CA), dismissing the claim for damages arising from his death, that there was no obligation to deprive him of his livelihood because he was not prepared to take care of himself in circumstances where he could well have done so.

Q Squiffy is an alcoholic employed by a brewery; he is frequently to be seen drunk on duty. He dies from alcoholic poisoning. His widow wishes to sue the brewery. Advise her.

12.10 Compliance with a statutory duty may not be enough

Bux v Slough Metals (1974)

The defendants had complied with a statutory duty to provide suitable goggles. However the defendants were held liable at *common law* as they had not insisted, by instruction and supervision, that the goggles *be worn*. Contributory negligence was assessed at 40%.

12.11 Servant is under an obligation to his master to use reasonable care and skill in the performance of his work

Lister v Romford Ice (1957)

The defendant servant whilst acting in the course of employment, carelessly reversed his master's lorry and knocked down his father, a fellow servant; his father, in another action, recovered damages from the master on the basis of the master's vicarious liability; the master was the plaintiff in the action to obtain an *indemnity* from the servant.

Held (HL) that the plaintiff *was* entitled to an indemnity from the defendant as the defendant was in breach of his implied duty to take reasonable care in the performance of his work.

12.12 If the master himself has been at fault, then the principle of *Lister* does not apply

Jones v Manchester Corporation (1952)

The Court of Appeal held that such an indemnity could not be claimed in the circumstances of that case. A recently qualified house surgeon started to anaesthetise a patient with nitrous oxide and then administered a full dose of pentothal to an already unconscious patient. The patient died.

Held (CA) that the hospital *itself* had been negligent in allowing a doctor of such slight experience to administer pentothal. It was considered that the fault of the inexperienced house surgeon was slight in comparison with the negligence of the hospital itself. Damages were apportioned 20% surgeon and 80% hospital.

13 Liability for chattels

13.1 A duty of care may exist to the ultimate transferee where there is an unknown danger

Per Lord Atkinson *Donoghue v Stevenson* (1932):

> A manufacturer of products which he sells in such a form as to show that he intends them to reach the ultimate consumer in the form in which they left him with no reasonable possibility of intermediate examination and with the knowledge that the absence of reasonable care in the preparation or putting up of the product will result in an injury to the consumer's life or property, owes a duty to the consumer to take that care.

This is the narrow ratio of that case.

13.1.1 Manufacturer

Liability has been imposed on a repairer.

Stennet v Hancock (1939)
An owner of a lorry took a wheel off the lorry for the defendant to repair; it was repaired and replaced on the lorry by the defendant; he was held liable when flange of wheel came adrift after the repair and injured the plaintiff, a pedestrian. The owner of the lorry was held to be not liable.

13.1.2 Products

Liability extends to articles other than 'manufactured' products.

Brown v Cotterill (1934)
The defendant carelessly erected a tombstone which fell on the plaintiff whilst she was arranging flowers on her grandmother's grave.

Held the defendant was liable under the principle of *Donoghue v Stevenson*.

13.1.3 In such a form

Grant v Australian Knitting Mills (1936)
A pair of pants was rendered dangerous by reason of an excess of sulphites used in their manufacture which caused the wearer to contract dermatitis.

Held (JCPC) that the manufacturers were liable; it mattered not that the pants were sent out in paper packets containing six pairs of which two were sold to the plaintiff; nor did it matter that had the plaintiff washed the pants before wearing them, the trouble would have been obviated. In the first place, mere possibility of interference did not affect liability; in the second place, it was not within the contemplation of the parties that the pants would have to be washed before being worn.

13.1.4 Ultimate consumer
A duty is owed to anyone whom the defendant ought reasonably to foresee as likely to be injured by the chattel.

Mason v Williams (1955)
A workman was injured in the eye by a splinter from a chisel he was using and which was manufactured by the defendant.

Held (CA) that he could recover damages against the defendant because he was the user of the chattel and was using it in the way it was intended to be used.

Hill v Crowe (1978)
The plaintiff, whilst loading a lorry, stood on a crate manufactured by the defendant; crate collapsed and the plaintiff was injured.

Held the defendant was liable because the crate was badly made; it should have been safe to stand on; it was likely that people such as the plaintiff would stand on it and be injured if it broke. It was no defence that the defendant had provided a good system and good supervision.

13.1.5 With no reasonable possibility of intermediate examination
The mere existence of an opportunity for intermediate examination is not enough.

Herschtal v Stewart & Arden (1939)
The defendant hired out a reconditioned car for the plaintiff's use; a wheel, carelessly fitted by the defendant's servant, came off and the plaintiff was injured.

Held the defendant liable; it could not reasonably be anticipated that there would be an intermediate examination of the car so as to reveal a carelessly fitted wheel; the car was intended for the plaintiff's immediate use.

Clay v Crump (1963)
The Court of Appeal held that where an unsafe wall had been left standing by demolition contractors they could not escape liability on the basis that subsequently building contractors would inspect the wall; as the wall had been left standing by experts, such examination was likely to be a cursory one, and so probably would not have revealed the defect.

Griffith v Arch Engineering Co (1968)

The plaintiff was lent a grinding tool by D1; the tool had been hired to D1 by D2; the tool was dangerous as it was set to revolve at too high a speed; when the plaintiff used it the tool burst.

Held, on the basis of reasonable foreseeability, that D1 and D2 were equally liable to the plaintiff, although he was guilty of contributory negligence of 20%. The mere possibility of intermediate examination did not exonerate D2 for D2 had no reason to suppose that D1 would make any independent examination of the tool.

13.1.6 Where the plaintiff has discovered the defect for himself, he may be without remedy

Farr v Butters (1932)

The defendant supplied a crane in parts which later had to be reassembled; the plaintiff's husband had the task of reassembly; he realised there were defects yet nevertheless he continued with his work; on using the completed crane he was killed as a result of the defect.

Held (CA) that there was not even a case to go to the jury.

Q Was *Farr v Butters* correctly decided?

13.1.7 Knowledge by the plaintiff will not debar him when he has no practicable alternative course open to him

Denny v Supplies and Transport (1950)

The defendant sent out a barge with timber so badly stowed that the plaintiff was injured when unloading.

Held the plaintiff could recover despite his realisation of the danger for there was no safe way of unloading badly stowed timber.

13.1.8 And with the knowledge that the absence of reasonable care in the preparation or putting up of the product

Hindustan SS v Siemens Bros Ltd (1955)

It was held that *Donoghue v Stevenson* applied to design which the plaintiff alleged constituted a trap. Defendant's engine room electric telegraph was installed by a sub contractor in the plaintiff's ship; the current was accidentally switched off with the result that the telegraph did not work, causing pointer to move to zero position, which engineer thought was 'full ahead'; engines were put full ahead and efforts by bridge to telegraph 'full astern' only rang bell which confirmed the engineer's belief that signal was truly 'full ahead'; ship rammed a tug and lock gates.

Held claim failed as the defendant could not then have reasonably foreseen that this sequence of events would occur. Further there were abundant opportunities for intermediate examination; the apparatus was installed by the plaintiff's agent who knew himself what would happen to the pointer if the current were switched off.

13.2 Consumer Protection Act 1987

The principle of strict liability was introduced by the Consumer Protection Act 1987, subject to a special limitation period of 10 years; any liability is extinguished 10 years after the product has been put into circulation. Liability in negligence at common law under the principle of *Donoghue v Stevenson* remains unaffected. Recourse to the common law will be necessary where the loss takes the form of damage to property not intended for private use – s 5(3) or where the special limitation period under the Act has expired.

14 Defamation

MORTIFICATION

14.1 Defamation is an attack on the plaintiff's reputation

14.1.1 'The statement must expose the plaintiff to hatred, ridicule or contempt in the mind of a reasonable man' *per* Baron Parke *Parmiter v Coupland* (1840)

14.1.2 'The statement must be a false statement about a man to his discredit' *per* Scrutton LJ *Youscoupoff v MGM* (1934)

14.1.3 'Would the words tend to lower the plaintiff in the estimation of right thinking members of society generally?' *per* Lord Atkin *Sim v Stretch* (1936)

The trial judge and a majority of the Court of Appeal had held the words complained of were defamatory of the plaintiff. The House of Lords held they were not.

Byrne v Dean (1937)

Held (CA 2–1) that an allegation that the plaintiff had informed the police about an illegal gambling machine in golf clubhouse was not capable of a defamatory meaning. Right thinking members of society would not think less of him – 'but he who gave the game away, may he Byrne in hell and rue the day'.

14.1.4 A corporation may sue for a libel affecting property, but not for one merely affecting personal reputation

Derbyshire CC v Times Newspapers Ltd (1993)

The plaintiff local authority sued publisher of *The Sunday Times* for articles which criticised the management and control of its superannuation fund. Defendant applied to have the action struck out as disclosing no cause of action against them.

Held (HL) that it should be struck out. Under common law a local authority did not have the right to maintain an action for damages for defamation as it would be contrary to the public interest for the organs of government, local or central, to have that right. It was of the highest public importance that a governmental body should be open to uninhibited public criticism. A right to sue for defamation would place an undesirable fetter on freedom of speech.

Bognor Regis UDC v Campion overruled.

Per Lord Keith:

A publication attacking the activities of the authority will necessarily be an attack on the body of councillors which represent the controlling party, or on the executives who carry out the day-to-day management of its affairs. If the individual reputation of any of these is wrongly impaired by the publication, any of these can himself bring proceedings for defamation.

14.2 Defamation does not necessarily involve an imputation of moral turpitude

Ridge v The English Illustrated Magazine (1913)
The defendant published a badly written story purporting to be written by the plaintiff.

Held this was capable of being defamatory.

Yousoupoff v MGM (1934)
The defendants made a film about the Russian Revolution. One scene depicted the rape of the plaintiff by Rasputin. This was untrue.

Held (CA) that it was defamatory falsely to allege that a woman had been raped. Arguably reasonable people would not shun the society of a woman who had had the misfortune to be raped but Slesser LJ dismissed the point with the remark 'It is to shut one's eyes to realities to make these nice [ie fine] distinctions.'

14.3 A publication has one natural meaning

Charleston v News Group Newspapers (1995)
In *News of the World* two photographs of the heads of the two plaintiffs, who played husband and wife in the television serial 'Neighbours' were superimposed on photographs of bodies engaged in intercourse or sodomy. Headline was 'Strewth! What's Harold up to with our Madge?' Plaintiffs alleged that photographs and headline were libellous because the ordinary and natural meaning was that the plaintiffs had posed for pornographic photographs. But captions under the photographs made it clear and text of accompanying article also made it clear that the photographs had been produced as part of a pornographic computer game in which plaintiffs' faces had been used *without* their knowledge or consent.

Held (HL) publications were *not* capable of the meanings pleaded in the Statement of Claim. A Plaintiff could not rely on a defamatory meaning only conveyed to the limited category of readers who only read the headlines.

Per Lord Bridge:

> But it would surely be even more destructive of the principle that a publication has 'the one and only meaning which the readers as reasonable men should have collectively understood the words to bear' to allow the plaintiff, without evidence, to invite the jury to infer that different groups of readers read different parts of the entire publication and for that reason understood it to mean different things, some defamatory, some not.'

14.4 The statement may have a secondary meaning – an innuendo

This may be a special or inferential meaning of words used – called a 'popular innuendo'.

Allsopp v Church of England Newspapers Ltd (1972)

The plaintiff complained of a statement published by the defendant that the plaintiff showed 'a preoccupation with the bent'.

Held (CA), on an interlocutory appeal, that the plaintiff should be required to give particulars of the inferential meaning which he said those words bore – what was the meaning of 'bent'?

14.5 An inferential meaning should not be left to the jury if a fair-minded man would not have drawn the inference

Lewis v The Daily Telegraph (1963)

The defendant reported that the fraud squad was enquiring into the affairs of the plaintiff; trial judge had left to the jury the possible meaning that the plaintiff was guilty of fraud.

Held (HL 4–1) that an ordinary man would not infer guilt from mere inquiry and that meaning should not have been left to the jury.

Q What inference could properly be drawn from the statement that X's affairs were the subject of investigation by the fraud squad?

14.6 The secondary meaning may arise from the statement complained of plus extrinsic facts, called legal innuendo

Tolley v Fry (1931)

The plaintiff was a well known amateur golfer; the defendant used the plaintiff's name, without permission, to advertise the defendant's chocolate.

Held (HL 4–1) that these facts supported the innuendo that the defendant had prostituted his amateur status and that that was defamatory.

Cassidy v Daily Mirror (1929)

The defendant published a picture of the plaintiff's husband accompanied by Miss X with the caption: 'Mr Cassidy and Miss X whose engagement has just been announced'.

Held (by CA) that the caption was capable of the bearing innuendo that the plaintiff was the mistress of Cassidy. It was immaterial that the defendant did not know of the special facts constituting the innuendo. But see now Defamation Act 1952 s 4 below.

Q Miss Take is well-known temperance worker. She is seen attending a meeting of Alcoholics Anonymous. Spite writes a letter to her employer complaining of this. Advise Miss Take.

14.7 There must be extrinsic facts

What has been said about the plaintiff by other people cannot be used to support an innuendo so long as the defendant himself has not repeated those other statements.

Astaire v Campling (1965)

The defendant said of the plaintiff that he was 'the man known in the fight game as Mr X', the plaintiff pleaded legal innuendo and set out, as the facts relied on, extracts from 14 newspapers or articles published by other persons. These articles were defamatory of 'Mr X'. Striking out the innuendo, the Court of Appeal *held* that to be actionable as libel, a statement must itself be false and defamatory of the plaintiff. Diplock LJ commented that if the plaintiff's contention were right:

... then any statement, however innocuous, about a plaintiff which would remind readers of his existence would be defamatory of him if, on recalling his existence, the reader might reasonably be expected to remember a defamatory statement which had been made about him by someone else, sometime before. In my view this is not the law of England.

14.8 Statement in permanent form is libel

By Defamation Act 1952 s 1 broadcasting of words by means of wireless telegraphy shall be treated as publication in permanent form. Section 16 provides 'words' includes pictures and visual images.

By Theatres Act 1968 s 4 the publication of words in the course of a performance of a play shall be treated as publication in permanent form. By section 7 this provision does not apply to a domestic performance in a private dwelling or to a rehearsal.

Osbourne v Boutler (1930)

The Court of Appeal held that a letter to the plaintiff defending quality of the defendant's beer was privileged (see below) and that this privilege was not lost by communication of its contents to shorthand typist and to X who had investigated the matter.

Held 2–1 that the communication to secretary and X would otherwise have been slander.

14.9 It is essential to every action for defamation that the words should refer to the plaintiff

14.9.1 Innocence is no defence at common law

Hulton v Jones (1910)

The defendant published a satirical article about how the English behaved abroad; the 'peg' of the article was a fictitious character – Artenus Jones; unknown to the author, there was a practising barrister named Artenus Jones and evidence was given that friends thought the article referred to him.

Held (HL) that the verdict for the plaintiff was justified; defamation was a fact and it was irrelevant that the defendant was ignorant of the plaintiff's existence.

By Defamation Act 1952 s 4 a person who publishes words 'innocently' in relation to the plaintiff may make an 'offer of amends'. If the offer is accepted and performed, no further action can be taken against the offer-or. If the offer is rejected, it is a defence to prove (1) the words were published 'innocently'; (2) that the offer was made as soon as practicable after the defendant had notice that the words were or might be defamatory of the plaintiff and that the offer had not been withdrawn; (3) if the words were not written by the defendant, that the author was without malice.

Ross v Hopkinson (1956)

It was held that an offer of amends made six weeks after receipt of complaint was not made as soon as practicable.

Words are published 'innocently' if: (i) the publisher did not intend to publish them concerning the plaintiff and did not know of circumstances by virtue of which they might be understood to refer to him; or (ii) the words were not defamatory on the face of them, and the publisher did not know of circumstances by virtue of which they might be understood to be defamatory of the plaintiff; and (iii) in either case the publisher exercised all reasonable care in relation to the publication.

Q Would *Hulton v Jones* and *Cassidy v Daily Mirror* be decided the same way today?

14.9.2 Defendant may be liable if he makes a statement which is true about A but is then taken to refer to B

Newstead v London Express (1939)
The defendant was held liable to the plaintiff when what he had written was true, but not true about the plaintiff; the plaintiff was sufficiently identified but not distinguished. 'Harold Newstead, 30-year-old Camberwell man' was reported as being convicted of bigamy; man in question was a barman. Plaintiff was Harold Newstead of Camberwell aged about 30 and a barber. Plaintiff awarded damages of one farthing.

Once again, see s 4.

14.9.3 There need not be something in the words themselves which point to the plaintiff

Morgan v Oldham Press (1971)
The plaintiff had been associating with a girl; the defendant published a statement that the girl had been kidnapped by dog-dopers; several witnesses thought it might refer to the plaintiff even though the girl's association seemed to be a free one.

Held (HL) that the statement could refer to the plaintiff. The result was that the publisher of a statement which identifies no-one is liable if knowledge of special facts – unknown to publisher – causes sensible people to think that the statement refers to the plaintiff.

Q Compare *Morgan* with *Astaire v Campling*, above.

14.9.4 Where defamatory statement reflects on a class, an individual member of that class cannot bring an action unless one of two criteria are satisfied

Knupffer v London Express (1944)
The plaintiff was a member of a society libelled by the defendant; there were 24 members in England and 2,000 in all; friends of the plaintiff who had read the libel took it as referring to him. The House of Lords held that a member of a libelled group had to show that either the group was so small that what was said of the group must refer to every member of it or

that there was something in the libel which singled out the plaintiff.

Held (HL) that in view of the size and distribution of the group, it was not reasonable, despite the evidence of the plaintiff's witnesses, to say that the plaintiff was libelled; there was nothing to point to him in particular.

14.10 Publication to a third person

Watt v Longsdon (1930)
The defendant showed a defamatory letter concerning the plaintiff to (i) chairman of company which employed them both (ii) wife of the plaintiff.

Held (CA) that communication of libel to the chairman was privileged as there was a reciprocal duty and interest in its communication. But communication to spouse of the plaintiff was not privileged and was an actionable publication.

14.11 Liability for republication

Vizetelly v Mudies Select Lending Library (1900)
It was held that a republisher is liable for his own act of publication unless he was acting as an innocent disseminator. He must then prove (a) he was innocent of any knowledge of the libel in the material distributed; (b) there were no circumstances which should have aroused his suspicion; (c) failure to discover was not due to any want of care on his part. In Vizetelly the defence of innocent dissemination failed as the defendant library had been negligent in failing to see a notice asking for withdrawal from circulation a book which libelled the plaintiff.

14.12 Original publisher not liable for republication unless he authorised or intended republication or if republication was the natural or probable consequence of the original publication

Derry v Handley (1867)
The defendant said of the plaintiff to X that she was 'a damned whore'; X repeated this to Y, his wife, who was the plaintiff's employer. Plaintiff was dismissed from Y's employment.

Held the defendant was liable for the republication.

Note ——

Note the immunity of X. Plaintiff's dismissal was vital to her claim as this case was prior to Slander of Woman Act 1891 which provided that an allegation of unchastity in a woman was actionable *per se*.

Slipper v BBC (1991)

The plaintiff, a detective chief superintendent flew out to Brazil to try to bring back to UK a convicted mail-train robber who had escaped. The attempt failed. BBC showed a film about the trip and the plaintiff claimed film portrayed him as an incompetent buffoon. He also claimed that reviews of the film repeated the 'sting' of the libel and that these reviews were relevant in assessing general damages to be awarded. BBC applied to have this further claim struck out. The Court of Appeal in an interlocutory appeal refused the application.

Held that an unauthorised repetition of a libel was normally novus actus interveniens and so too remote. Nevertheless, where appropriate, on particular facts, repetition of the sting of a libel by an unauthorised third party would be treated as the natural and probable consequence of the original publication so as to expose the original publisher to a claim for damages in respect of the repetition. This was a question of remoteness of damage and raised an issue of fact for the jury. Accordingly there was no case for striking out the plaintiff's claim.

14.13 Justification is a defence – that the statement is true

Wakely v Cooke (1894)

The plaintiff was a coroner and the defendant wrote that 'there can be no court of justice unpolluted which this libellist journalist ... is allowed to disgrace with his presidentship.' Defendant attempted to justify 'libellous journalist' by saying that as proprietor of *The Lancet* he had in fact published one libel.

Held that a charge of general bad conduct could not be justified by proof of a single instance of bad conduct. The plea of justification failed as the statement meant that the plaintiff was an habitual libeller.

Alexander v NE Railway (1865)

The plaintiff had been sentenced to a fine or 14 days imprisonment; the defendant reported this as a fine or 21 days imprisonment.

Held it was sufficient if the defendant could prove that the 'sting' of statement was true although some detail was untrue. Defence of justification succeeded as there was evidence that the statement was substantially true.

By Defamation Act 1952 s 5 in an action for defamation in respect of words containing two or more distinct charges against the plaintiff, a degree of justification shall not fail by reason only that the truth of every charge is not proved if the words not proved to be true do not materially injure the plaintiff's reputation having regard to the truth of the remaining charges.

By Civil Evidence Act 1968 s 13 in an action for defamation, proof that a person stands convicted of criminal offence is conclusive evidence that he committed the offence.

Q Badger said of Toad 'He is the most frightful road hog. Further, he drinks too much.' Toad was convicted last year or speeding and was fined £20. Advise Toad.

14.14 Fair comment: it is a defence that the statement is fair comment made in good faith on a matter of public interest

14.14.1 The test of fairness

Silkin v Beaverbrook Newspapers (1958)
The defendant criticised the plaintiff who had opposed West Germany rearmament and then shortly afterwards arranged the import of German 'bubble' cars. Diplock J, addressing the jury, said:

> Was this an opinion however exaggerated, obstinate or prejudiced which was honestly held by the writer ... Could a fair-minded man have been capable of writing this?

Jury returned a verdict for the defendant.

Slim v The Daily Telegraph (1968)
D1 published two letters written by D2 criticising the conduct of the plaintiffs. P1 as town clerk had forbidden vehicular traffic down a certain path; later as legal adviser to P2 he had tried to establish right of way for such traffic.

Held (CA) that even if the words complained of did impute dishonesty and hypocrisy – which probably they did not – the defence of fair comment was available and succeeded. Writer had got his facts right and had honestly stated his real opinion on a matter of public interest.

14.14.2 To impute motive is to make a statement of fact and so must be justified

Campbell v Spottiswode (1863)
The defendant accused the plaintiff of 'puffing' his newspaper by a false pretence that he was propagating the Gospel in China.

Held such an allegation had to be justified; there was no truth in it and so the plaintiff succeeded in his claim.

14.14.3 Words complained of must be related to some facts

Kemsley v Foot (1952)

The defendant attacked the Beaverbrook press; the only reference to Kemsley – another newspaper proprietor – was in the heading to the article 'lower than Kemsley'. This remarkedly short statement went to the House of Lords on an interlocutory appeal; the plaintiff alleged libel and the defendant pleaded fair comment.

Held (HL) that the defence of fair comment should be allowed; the statement was capable of being fair comment. There must be 'a sufficient substratum of facts stated or indicated' *per* Lord Porter. Held that sufficient substratum of fact was indicated, Lords Kemsley and Beaverbrook were both well-known newspaper proprietors.

14.14.4 Defamation Act 1952 s 6

This provides that a plea of fair comment shall not fail by reason only that the truth of every allegation of fact is not proved:

> if the expression of opinion is fair comment having regard to such of the facts alleged or referred to in the words complained of, as are proved.

London Artists Ltd v Littler (1969)

The defendant wrote a letter, made available to the national press, alleging a conspiracy to close a West End play. On appeal, the only issue was that of fair comment.

Held (CA) that the fate of the play was a matter of public interest; however the allegation of a plot was a statement of fact, in itself defamatory of the plaintiff, which was not reasonably capable of being considered as comment.

Per Lord Denning MR:

> If in his original article he sets out basic facts which are themselves defamatory of the plaintiff, then he must prove them to be true; and this is the case just as much after s 6 as it was before.

14.14.5 Defence of fair comment will fail if the defendant was actuated by express malice

Thomas v Bradbury Agnew (1906)

The defendant published a book review by X, it was found that X had a personal spite against the plaintiff; there was extrinsic evidence of malice.

Held (CA) that it was proper for judge to invite jury to take evidence of malice into account in deciding whether comment was fair; that review was distorted by malice. Although the defence was shared by the rest of the public, it was on individual right and therefore it was no defence that someone else might have written the same review without malice – it was the individual who was sued.

Telnikoff v Matsuevitch (1991)

The plaintiff, a Russian émigré, wrote an article published in a newspaper, in which he criticised the BBC's Russian service for recruiting too many employees from ethnic minorities of the Soviet Union. Defendant, also a Russian émigré, was incensed by the article and wrote a letter, published in the same newspaper, complaining that the article was racist and anti-Semitic. Plaintiff claimed letter to be defamatory; the defendant pleaded fair comment on a matter of public interest, not justification; the plaintiff then alleged that the defendant was actuated by express malice.

Held (HL) that the court had to construe letter on its own when deciding whether words complained of were a defamatory statement of fact rather than comment. A reasonable jury looking at the letter alone could properly find that letter contained a statement of fact: the question whether it was fact or comment should have been left to the jury.

Per Lord Templeman:

> In my opinion fact or comment depends on the true construction of the letter and not on the true construction of the article. If in the letter the defendant made allegations of fact, those allegations cannot be converted into comment by the article written by the plaintiff.

Secondly, the defendant who relied on fair comment did not have to show that the comment was an honest expression of his own views but merely that the comment was based on true facts and fair in that any man, however prejudiced or obstinate, could honestly have held the views expressed.

Per Lord Keith:

> The law is correctly stated in Gatley on Libel and Slander 'In alleging any unfairness the plaintiff takes on him or herself the onus, also taken by an allegation of malice, to prove that the criticism is unfair either from the language used or from some extraneous circumstance'.

On the facts there was no evidence of express malice fit to go to the jury.

14.15 Absolute privilege

When this defence is invoked, defendant is claiming that the statement complained of is not actionable.

Statements made by senior officers of state in the course of their official duties

Chatterton v Secretary of State for India (1895)

Plaintiff was an officer in the Indian Staff Corps; he complained that the defendant had conveyed in writing to the Parliamentary Under Secretary of State for India an untrue statement affecting plaintiff's reputation. Defendant had, in the course of duty, written to the Under Secretary stating that the Commander in Chief in India recommended the removal of the plaintiff to the half pay list as an officer. The statement was made to enable him to answer a question in the House of Commons.

CA dismissed plaintiff's appeal from the decision of the judge in chambers that the action should be dismissed as vexatious.

Per Lord Esher:

> What is the reason for the existence of this law? It does not exist for the benefit of the official. All judges have said that the ground of its existence is the injury to the public good which would result if such an inquiry were allowed as would be necessary if the action were maintainable. An inquiry would take away from the public official his freedom of action in a matter concerning the public welfare, because he would have to appear before a jury and be cross examined as to his conduct. That would be contrary to the interest of the public, and the privilege is, therefore, absolute in regard to the contents of such a document as that upon which this action is founded.

Note the difference between this meaning of 'privilege' and the privilege that can be claimed under the law of *evidence*. When a party claims privilege according to the law of evidence, he claims that a document need not be produced or that a question need not be answered. In defamation, the statement in question is already before the court; the question is – *can it be sued upon?*

14.16 Qualified privilege

It is a defence to establish that the statement complained of was made on an occasion of qualified privilege

14.16.1 A moral duty is sufficient to establish privilege

Stuart v Bell (1891)
The defendant was host to the explorer, Stanley; the defendant informed him that his valet, the plaintiff was a thief; Stanley dismissed the plaintiff who sued the defendant in slander.

Held (CA 2–1) that the defendant's plea of qualified privilege succeeded.

14.16.2 Mere belief in the existence of a duty is not sufficient

Watt v Longsdon (1930)
The defendant believed that he had a duty to inform the plaintiff's wife of matters concerning the plaintiff's conduct.

Held (CA) no such duty existed.

14.16.3 A common interest will establish the defence

Bryanston v De Vries (1973)

The defendant became dissatisfied with the plaintiff's company and wrote a letter to shareholders; the plaintiff received a copy and gained an interim injunction so that the letters were in fact never sent out to the shareholders. Plaintiff claimed that there had been a non-privileged communication to the typist and photocopier.

Held (CA 2–1) that the communication was privileged as dictation to the typist and handling of letter to photocopier was the accepted mode of writing the documents; further, there was a sufficient common interest in seeing that the usual course of business was successful. *Osborne v Boulter* (1930) followed.

14.16.4 The only kind of recklessness which destroys qualified privilege is indifference to the truth or falsity of the statement

Horrocks v Lowe (1974)

The defendant councillor slandered the plaintiff councillor at a council meeting; it was accepted that the occasion was subject to qualified privilege; the defendant had jumped to conclusions which were irrational.

Held (HL) that the defendant's honest belief in the truth of what he was saying on that privileged occasion entitled him to succeed in his defence of qualified privilege.

14.16.5 MP has an interest in receiving from a constituent a complaint about a public official or professional man acting in the constituency

Beach v Freeson (1971)

Held (CA) that MP the defendant succeeded in his defence; he had written letters, admittedly defamatory of the plaintiff solicitors, to the Law Society and to the Lord Chancellor, following complaints from his constituents. There was a moral duty to report and the Law Society and Lord Chancellor had a reciprocal interest in hearing the complaint.

14.16.6 Certain fair and accurate reports published in newspapers Defamation Act 1952 s 7 or broadcast in UK s 9

These reports include police or government notices issued for public information. Information given by a press officer of a government department is not a government notice under s 7 when not in a formal statement issued on the initiative of a government department – *Blackshaw v Lord* (1983). The result was that the defendant could not rely on information given to him over the telephone by a government press officer. Defendant was a journalist of *The Daily Telegraph*. Plaintiff's name was not given in the original communication but was given in the defendant's press report which alleged incompetence at the Department of Energy. The Court of Appeal held that common law privilege did not apply as there was no duty to make the plaintiff's name known to the public. Jury award of £45,000 damages to the plaintiff upheld.

14.16.7 Malice defeats the defence of qualified privilege but the malice of the master or principal is *not* imputed to the servant or agent

Egger v Viscount Chelmsford (1964)

A committee of the Kennel Club issued a letter defamatory of the plaintiff who was a long established judge in dog shows; there was a history of discord in the Club; some members of the committee were actuated by malice.

Held (CA) that the innocent committee members were entitled severally to the protection of qualified privilege as also was the innocent secretary who had written the letter.

Q Mr Grouser, a member of the Dingle Dell cricket club, is incensed by what he believes to be ball tampering by Speed, the team's fast bowler. At a committee meeting Mr Grouser, proposes the expulsion of Speed. The previous fast bowler, Torpid, is highly delighted. The decision is taken by the committee to expel Speed for ball tampering. Scribe, the club secretary, dictates the letter of dismissal to his wife. Advise Speed.

15 Vicarious liability

15.1 The relationship of master and servant, often now described as employer and employee, may give rise to vicarious liability; it is a contract of service

Stevenson v MacDonald (1952)

Per Denning LJ:

It is often easy to recognise a contract of service when you see it, but difficult to say wherein the difference lies. A ship's master, a chauffeur, and a reporter on the staff of a newspaper are all employed under a contract of service; but a ship's pilot, a taximan and a newspaper contributor are employed under a contract for services. One feature which seems to run through the instances is that, under a contract of service, a man is employed as part of the business and his work is done as an integral part of the business; whereas, under a contract for services, his work, although done for the business, is not integrated into it but is only accessory to it.

15.2 Medical staff are deemed to be servants

Collins v Herts CC (1947)

On the night before an operation a house surgeon rang up the surgeon, who was to perform the operation, for his instructions; the surgeon gave instructions for a solution of procaine, a local anaesthetic, to be prepared; the house surgeon misheard this and procured a solution of cocaine; the hospital pharmacist took this order by word of mouth and supplied, without taking steps to verify that no mistake had been made, an unheard of dosage for an injection of cocaine. The surgeon took no steps to check that the solution was what he had ordered, injected the cocaine and the patient died.

Held the pharmacist and the house surgeon were both negligent and the hospital was vicariously liable for their negligence. But the hospital was not liable for the surgeon, a part-time consultant who was *himself* negligent.

Razzel v Snowball (1954)

A part time consultant at a National Health Service hospital was held to be entitled to the protection conferred by Limitation Act 1939 s 21 – now repealed – in respect of acts done in pursuance of any Act of Parliament or any public duty or authority.

   Per Denning LJ:

> It is the duty of the Minister to provide all necessary services at the hospitals.
> He is to do it by means of doctors and nurses under paragraph (b) and by means
> of specialists under paragraph (c). He does not discharge his duty merely by
> appointing competent doctors and nurses and competent specialists. He has not
> merely to provide the staff. He has to provide their services; and inasmuch as
> their services consist of treating the sick it is his duty to treat the sick by means
> of their services.

Q Is Denning LJ – as he then was – describing primary or secondary liability?

15.3 Course of employment

15.3.1 A wrongful act falls within the scope of employment if it is either a wrongful act authorised by the master or a wrongful mode of doing some act authorised by the master

Kay v ITW (1967)

Defendant's servant tried to return his fork-lift truck to a warehouse; a
large lorry was in the way and so the servant attempted to move the lorry;
it went backwards, injuring the plaintiff

   Held (CA) this was within the scope of employment, despite the servant's
folly; he was attempting to return the truck which *was* part of his duties.

Jefferson v Derbyshire Farms Ltd (1921)

Servant, aged 16, was ordered by his employer to fill some tins with petrol
from a drum; whilst doing this he lit a cigarette and threw the match on
the floor. The garage was destroyed in the resultant fire.

   Held (CA), dismissing the appeal, that the employers were vicariously
liable.

   Per Warrington LJ:

> It was in the scope of his employment to fill the tin with motor spirit from the
> drum. That work required special precautions. The act which caused the dam-
> age was an act done while he was engaged in this dangerous operation, and it
> was an improper act in the circumstances. That is to say, the boy was doing the
> work of his employers in an improper way and without taking reasonable pre-
> cautions; and in that case the employers are liable.

Century Insurance Ltd v Northern Ireland Road Transport Board (1942)

Driver of a petrol tanker, an employee of the defendants, was delivering
petrol to the plaintiff's garage. Whilst transferring petrol to an underground tank he lit a cigarette and threw match to the ground.

   Held (HL) that the act of lighting a cigarette was for his own comfort and
convenience; nevertheless the House of Lords declined to treat it as a separate act; in the circumstances it was to be viewed as an improper mode of

carrying out his task of delivering petrol.

Per Lord Wright:

The act of a workman in lighting his pipe or cigarette is an act done for his own comfort and convenience and at least, generally speaking, not for his employer's benefit. That last condition, however, is no longer essential to fix liability on the employer (*Lloyd v Grace Smith and Co*). Nor is such an act *prima facie* negligent. It is in itself both innocent and harmless. The negligence is to be found by considering the time when and the circumstances in which the match is struck and thrown down. The duty of the workman to his employer is so to conduct himself in doing his work as not negligently to cause damage either to the employer himself or his property or to third persons or their property, and thus to impose the same liability on the employer as if he had been doing the work himself and committed the illegal act. This may seem too obvious as a matter of common sense to require either argument or authority. I think that what plausibility the contrary argument might seem to possess results from treating the act of lighting the cigarette in abstraction from the circumstances as a separate act.

General Engineering Services Ltd v Kingston & St Andrews Corporation (1988)

Fire broke out in the plaintiff's premises; local fire brigade was called out but took five times the normal time to reach fire; brigade was operating a 'go slow' policy as part of industrial action in supporting a pay claim. By the time engine arrived, stopping and starting, the plaintiff's property was destroyed. JCPC held that the mode and manner of brigade's driving to the fire was not a wrongful and unauthorised mode of doing an act authorised by its employees, which was to drive as expeditiously as possible to the scene of the fire. It was not a mode of performing the authorised act at all. Therefore their conduct was *outside* the fire brigade's course of employment. The local authority was thus *not* liable for the default of the brigade.

Q Timid is driving a fire engine to a reported fire; he drives very slowly because he is determined not to have an accident. By the time the fire engine arrives, the fire is out of control. Livid is the owner of the house on fire and seeks compensation. Advise him.

15.3.2 Course of employment – commencement

Compton v McClure (1975)

D1 was late for work; he drove on to the premises of D2, his employer, at too fast a speed and negligently injured the plaintiff.

Held the employers were vicariously liable.

Per May J:

I find myself driven to the conclusion that the least artificial place at which to draw the line in the circumstances of the present case is the boundary of the factory premises; at the gates where employees coming in find control by the employers starts; where the 5 mph speed limit begins; where there are security officers to see that the traffic is proceeding properly; where employees at this point are clearly coming to work – providing, of course, that that is the purpose for which they cross the boundary ... I have come to the conclusion in the present case that the second defendants must be held to be vicariously liable for the clear negligence of the first the defendant and, accordingly, that there must be judgment for the plaintiff against both the defendants for whatever sum I consider to be the appropriate award by way of damages.

15.3.3   Course of employment – continuance

Smith v Stages (1989)

Plaintiff and D1 were peripatetic laggers employed by D2. P and D1 were taken off a job in the Midlands and were sent to an urgent job in Wales. The two employees were paid eight hours travelling time and eight hours for the return journey plus their rail fare. No stipulation was made as to their mode of travel. They travelled in D1's car. At the end of the job, after working 24 hours without break they decided, instead of sleeping, to go straight back to the Midlands. On the way back D1's car left the road and crashed through a brick wall. Plaintiff sued D1 for negligence and D2 on the basis of vicarious liability. Driver was uninsured and the MIB agreement did not apply as time limits for bringing an action had not been complied with.

Held (HL) that D2 were vicariously liable for D1's negligence. An employee, who *for a short time* was required by his employer to work at a different place of work, *was* acting in the course of employment when returning, if he travelled back in the employer's time which he *would* be doing if he were paid wages for the time travelled. Since employees *had* been paid while driving back to the Midlands, they had been travelling in employer's time and employers were vicariously liable for DI's negligence.

Per Lord Lowry:

The paramount rule is that an employee travelling on the highway will be acting in the course of his employment if, and only if, he is at the material time going about his employer's business. One must not confuse the duty to turn up for one's work with the concept of already being 'on duty' while travelling to it.

Vandyke v Fender (1970) approved.

Per Lord Denning MR:

When a man is going to or coming from work, along a public road as a passenger in a vehicle provided by his employer, he is not then in the course of his employment – unless he is *obliged* by the terms of his employment to travel on that vehicle.

Per Lord Lowry:

What was said here about the passenger in relation to the course of his employment was also apposite to the driver.

15.3.4 Master is not liable when servant is in a 'frolic of his own'

Storey v Ashton (1869)

Defendant's carman – a driver – delivered some wine; he was then due to bring back some empty casks to his employers; on the return journey he deviated from the route to collect wine for a friend; whilst on that deviation he drove negligently, injuring the plaintiff.

Held the defendant not liable.

15.3.5 Express prohibition by master may be no defence

Limpus v LGO (1862)

Driver of the defendant's bus had printed instructions not to race or obstruct other buses; in defiance of this order the driver obstructed a rival bus and caused a collision.

Held the defendant liable *irrespective* of any prohibition because the driver in question was employed to drive and to promote his masters business; his act therefore was merely a wrongful mode of doing those authorised things.

Rose v Plenty (1976)

The Court of Appeal held 2-1 that where the defendant's servant, a milkman, gave a prohibited lift to an unauthorised passenger, the plaintiff, and accepted prohibited assistance in delivering milk, there *was* vicarious liability for the driver's negligence. The passenger, aged 13, was in fact helping driver to deliver milk when injured by the negligent driving of the milk-float.

Held (CA) that that put the forbidden act within the sphere of employment because it was for the *purposes* of the employer.

Limpus v LGO followed.

Practical effect of *Rose* is now limited because since 1971 there is compulsory insurance for passenger risk and so the question of employer's liability will not be in issue so long as the *driver* is at fault.

15.3.6 Effect of prohibition may be to define the limits of employment

Iqbal v London Transport Executive (1973)

Defendant's servant was a bus conductor; in defiance of the defendant's prohibition – by notice and by rule book – he drove a bus which was blocking his bus; he injured the plaintiff who was in fact his own driver.

Held there was no vicarious liability as the driving was not within the sphere of his employment as a *conductor*.

Iqbal was discussed in *Rose v Plenty*.

Per Lord Denning MR:

Iqbal v London Transport Executive seems to be out of line and should be regarded as decided on its own special circumstances.

Per Scarman LJ:

In that case the Court of Appeal had to consider whether the London Transport Executive was liable for the action of a bus conductor in driving contrary to his express instructions a motor bus a short distance in a garage. Of course, the court had no difficulty at all in distinguishing between the spheres of employment of a driver and conductor in the London Transport. Accordingly, it treated the prohibition upon the conductors acting as drivers of motor buses as a prohibition which defined their sphere of employment.

Q Consider whether *Iqbal* was correctly decided.

15.3.7 Basis of vicarious liability is implied authority

Keppel Bus v Ahmad (1974)

Plaintiff was a passenger on the defendant's bus; whilst the conductor was collecting fares he was rude to the plaintiff and hit him over the head with his ticket machine.

Held (JCPC) that the defendant was not vicariously liable as conductor did not have implied authority to act as he did; there was no emergency situation and as 'manager' of the bus it could not be said that his act was an act of management.

Petterson v Royal Oak Hotel Ltd (1948) NZ LR 136

Barman refused to serve a customer who thereupon threw a glass at the barman; the barman picked up a piece of the broken glass and threw it at the customer; a piece of the glass struck a bystander in the eye.

Held that the employer of barman *was* vicariously liable; keeping order was part of his duties and he was doing that in an improper way.

Q Squirt is a petrol attendant; he believes that a motorist, Splash, has not paid for his petrol and attempts to prevent him from leaving; there is a heated altercation and Squirt punches Splash. Advise Gazzo, owner of the petrol station.

15.3.8 A dishonest act may be the basis of vicarious liability

Lloyd v Grace Smith (1912)

The House of Lords *held* that the defendant solicitor was responsible for the fraud of his managing clerk. Plaintiff had sought advice on her financial affairs and was seen by the managing clerk; he perpetrated the fraud for his own financial gain. The Court of Appeal had held that his master was thus not responsible but the House of Lords held that he *was* the responsibility of his employer, *whatever* the motive for the fraud.

Per Earl Loreburn:

If the agent commits the fraud purporting to act in the course of business such as he was authorised or *held out* as authorised, to transact on account of his principal, then the latter may be held liable for it.

Morris v Martin (1965)

Plaintiff had sent her fur coat to X for cleaning; by a sub-bailment he sent the coat to the defendant for the actual work to be done; the coat was then stolen by one of the cleaners.

Held (CA) that the defendant had, as a bailee, a duty to take reasonable care of the bailed goods; if that duty were entrusted to a servant or agent, then the bailee was answerable for the manner in which that servant or agent carried out his duty. The decision was, in part, based on a primary duty owed by a bailee.

Per Lord Denning MR:

If you go through the cases on this difficult subject, you will find that, in the ultimate analysis, they depend on the nature of the duty owed by the master towards the person whose goods have been lost or damaged. If the master is under a duty to use due care to keep goods safely and protect them from theft and depredation, he cannot get rid of his responsibility by delegating his duty to another. If he entrusts that duty to his servant, he is answerable for the way in which the servant conducts himself therein. No matter whether the servant be negligent, fraudulent, or dishonest, the master is liable.

Note ────────────────────────────────

X, if sued, would have been sued in *contract*; an exemption clause – as the law then stood – would have prevented the plaintiff from suing X. But that exemption clause did not prevent her from suing the defendant in *tort*; *his* exemption clause was only effective as against X.

─────────────────────────────────────

Q Fluff takes her diamond ring to a jeweller, Flash, to be cleaned. Char, a tea lady, sees the ring on a work bench and takes it home. Advise Fluff.

15.3.9 Even skylarking may be within the course of employment

Harrison v Michelin Tyre Co (1985)

X, in the ordinary course of his employment, was wheeling a trolley along a passage way when he pushed the edge of the trolley under a duck board on which the plaintiff was standing; the plaintiff fell and was injured.

Held that the employer was vicariously liable; that act of horseplay was 'part and parcel' of his employment.

15.4 Employer and independent contractor

15.4.1 An employer will be responsible for the acts of his independent contractor if he authorised him to do an illegal act

Ellis v Sheffield Gas Consumers Co (1853)
Employers engaged a contractor to dig, without authority, a trench for gas pipes. That was a public nuisance.

Held the employer was liable when the plaintiff was injured falling over the pile of stones produced in consequence and carelessly left.

15.4.2 An employer has a personal responsibility to see that proper instructions are issued

Robinson v Beaconsfield RC (1911)
Employer was held responsible for his independent contractor's action of dumping sewage on the plaintiff's land; no instructions had been given as to the proper disposal of the sewage; employer then was held liable for damage caused by the failure to issue those proper instructions.

15.4.3 There are seven exceptional cases where an employer will be responsible for damage caused by an independent contractor

- *Rylands v Fletcher* (1868)
- Operations on or adjoining the highway – *Tarry v Ashton* (1876)
- Where work involves the use of fire – *Balfour v Barty-King* (1957)
- Breach of common law duty of employer to his servant – *Wilson and Clyde Coal v English* (1938)
- Where nuisance was the inevitable consequence of the operation – *Matania v National Provincial Bank* (1936)
- Statutory duty where duty is absolute *Smith v Cammell Laird* (1940)
- Where extra hazardous activities are involved

Honeywell & Stein v Larkin Bros (1934)
Plaintiff employed the defendant to take flashlight photographs of cinema, igniting magnesium powder in a metal tray; the cinema curtains caught fire and cinema was damaged; the plaintiff satisfied cinema owner's claim and then sought an indemnity from the defendant.

Held the plaintiff was so entitled as he was liable for the defendant's negligence.

15.4.4 An employer is never responsible for the 'collateral negligence' of an independent contractor or his servants

Padbury v Holliday (1912)
Defendant, who was building premises adjacent to highway, employed a sub-contractor to install windows; an employee of this subcontractor put a

tool on a window sill; later the window was blown shut and tool fell off sill, hitting the plaintiff.

Held the defendant was *prima facie* liable as the work was adjacent to the highway; but the defendant was not liable as the injury was caused by an act of collateral negligence, ie negligence which was not necessarily incident to the work delegated to be done.

15.4.5 No liability for an independent contractor working near a highway

Salsbury v Woodland (1969)

D1 employed a contractor D2 to cut down a tree in D1's garden; the tree stood 28ft from the road; the work was done negligently, the tree hit telephone wires which landed in the road. Plaintiff intended to coil up wire but, on seeing D3 approaching too fast in his car, flung himself to the ground to avoid being hurt by the wires; he was injured by the fall. The Court of Appeal held D1 was not liable for his independent contractor. The authorities were concerned with work being done *in* a highway, *not* near a highway. D1's appeal was allowed.

15.4.6 Special cases

Parent and child: a parent may be directly liable for his own negligence in giving his child the opportunity to inflict harm

Bebee v Sales (1916)

A father gave his son an air gun; despite some trouble over the gun, father continued to allow his son to use the gun; son shot the plaintiff in the eye.

Held that the parent was negligent in allowing his child to have such a gun after receiving warnings of the danger.

Gorely v Codd (1966)

A child once more shot the plaintiff using an air gun.

Held that the parent was *not liable* as adequate instruction in the use of the gun had in fact been given. However, there was negligence on the part of the minor and *he* was held liable for the plaintiff's injury.

Q Gormless buys a pea shooter for his son, Simon. Simon shoots peas at Prudence and a pea hits her in the eye damaging it. Advise Prudence.

Surgeons and staff: surgeon has no vicarious liability for the negligence of hospital staff

Morris v Winsbury White (1937)

Held that a surgeon who had performed an operation for prostate trouble could not be held responsible for any negligence by the nurses or the hospital medical officers in performing routine post-operational tasks such as shortening and re-inserting drainage tubes; there was no duty upon the surgeon to attend during the performance of routine tasks of that nature.

A surgeon will be responsible for his own negligence in not checking the accuracy of the operating staff.

Collins v Herts CC (1947)

A consultant surgeon injected an incorrect anaesthetic as a result of a house surgeon having misunderstood telephoned instructions.

Held that the consultant surgeon was *directly* responsible for his *own* negligence in failing to carry out *some* check.

McCarey v Associated Newspapers (1964)

It was held to be *defamatory* to suggest falsely that a surgeon had blamed a theatre sister for handing him an incorrect solution for injection; he had in fact accepted responsibility for the solution he had injected.

Ownership of car: vicarious liability does not flow from ownership of car

Samson v Aitchison (1912)

Defendant was about to sell his car to X; he let X take a test run but stayed in the car. Plaintiff was injured by X's negligent driving. Held that as owner of the car was still in possession and occupation of the car, he was to be held liable as *principal* for the damage caused by the negligence of the person actually driving.

Where owner of car not in occupation, liability stems from the delegation of a task.

Hewitt v Bonvin (1940)

Son had borrowed his father's car for the son's *private* purposes.

Held (CA) that liability did not depend on ownership but on the delegation of a task or duty. Held that the father, as owner of the car, was *not* liable.

Ormrod v Crossville (1953)

X intended to take part in the Monte Carlo rally and then to go on holiday with Mr and Mrs Ormrod; the arrangement was that the Ormrods would drive X's holiday car to Monte Carlo and then the car would be used for their joint holiday. The Ormrods set off early to spend a little time in France but they soon ran into a bus owned by the defendant.

Held (CA) that X was liable for the negligence of Mr Ormrod although that first part of the trip was for the Ormsrod's enjoyment, a *mixture of purpose was sufficient.*

Per Denning LJ:

> The law puts an especial responsibility on the owner of a vehicle who allows it out on the road in charge of someone else, no matter whether it is his servant, friend, or anyone else. If it is being used wholly or partly on the owner's business or for the owner's purposes, then the owner is liable for any negligence on

the part of the driver. The owner only escapes liability when he lends it out or hires it out to a third person to be used for purposes in which the owner has no interest or concern.

Morgans v Launchbury (1972)

The owner of a car allowed her husband to drive it; he had promised her that if he had had too much to drink he would get someone else to drive him home. One night, after a drinking session, he asked X to drive him home; X drove negligently, injuring the plaintiff.

Held (HL) that the wife was *not* vicariously liable for the negligence of X, although the husband *was*. The arrangement between husband and wife could not be described as a delegation of a task or duty; it was no more than the kind of assurance that any responsible husband would give to his wife.

Per Lord Wilberforce:

I regard it as clear that in order to fix vicarious liability on the owner of a car in such a case as the present, it must be shown that the driver was using it for the owner's purposes, under delegation of a task or duty. The substitution for this clear conception of a vague test based on 'interest' or 'concern' has nothing in reason or authority to commend it. Every man who gives permission for the use of his chattel may be said to have an interest or concern in its being carefully used, and, in most cases if it is a car, to have an interest or concern in the safety of the driver, but it has never been held that mere permission is enough to establish vicarious liability.

Borrowed servants: when the general employer of a servant lends him to another employer – the special employer – whose servant is he?

Mersey Docks Board v Coggins & Griffiths (1947)

The House of Lords held that the onus was on the general employer to show that vicarious responsibility had been shifted on to the special employer and that the onus was a heavy one. The general employer had hired a crane to a special employer, the defendant stevedores, and provided the crane driver; he negligently injured X; the *contractual* term was that the driver should be the servant of the special employer; the stevedores could tell him what to do but not how to operate the crane.

Held (HL) that as special employer had no power of control over driver's management of the crane, the servant *remained* the servant of the general employer.

White v Tarmac (1967)

The House of Lords *held* that the general employers were 100% liable to the plaintiff in *tort*; but in contract, on its particular terms, they were entitled to an *indemnity* from the special employer.

Q It is more satisfactory, from the plaintiff's point of view, to be able to sue the general employer. Why should this be so?

16 Trespass to land

16.1 The plaintiff

16.1.1 Actual possession of land suffices against any person wrongfully entering land

Harper v Charlesworth (1825)

The plaintiff had possession of Crown lands; the defendant purported to exercise a public right of way on that land.

Held the plaintiff could sue the defendant in trespass although the Crown might, at any time, have removed the plaintiff from that possession.

Per Holroyd J:

> An entry on the possession of another cannot be justified, unless it is made by the authority of a person in whom the right of soil is vested.

Delaney v Smith (1946)

Plaintiff's possession was held to be insufficient *as against* the defendant, who could show that *he* was the person entitled to immediate possession as against the plaintiff. There was a lease which did not comply with the Law of Property Act 1925 s 40.

Held that lessee who had been ejected could not have an action for trespass against lessor.

Fowley Marine v Gifford (1968)

The Court of Appeal expressly refused to consider the matter of title. Plaintiff succeeded against the defendant in an action for trespass to land on the issue of *possession*. Plaintiff had showed sufficient *prior* acts of possession to succeed against the defendant; the acts of possession were done as an assertion of ownership; any act of the defendant was not equivalent to that, and so could not be regarded as acts of concurrent possession.

16.1.2 If land has been demised, it is the tenant who has the right to sue for trespass

Baxter v Taylor (1832)

Defendant, exercising a purported right of way, entered upon land with horse and cart and deposited stones.

Held that the plaintiff, as landlord, had no claim; he had no right of immediate possession and so could not complain of the immediate trespass; his only right to sue was for an act injurious to the *reversion* and the deposit of stones did not damage *that*.

16.1.3   Plaintiff must have the right of exclusive possession

Abbeyfield Society v Woods (1968)
Plaintiff society provided sheltered accommodation; it wished the defendant, a blind person, to vacate his room and to seek hospital care.

Held (CA) that the defendant had a mere licence and so had no right to exclusive possession. It made no difference that he paid a regular sum described as 'rent'. Thus he was not entitled to stay, his licence had been lawfully revoked.

16.2   Forms of trespass
It must be a *direct* form of interference. It is actionable *per se*.

16.2.1   (1) Personal entry

League Against Cruel Sports v Scott (1985)
Plaintiffs owned various areas of unfenced moorland around Exmoor for the purpose of establishing a deer sanctuary. Hunting was not allowed on this land. Defendants were joint masters of the Devon and Somerset staghounds; on a number of occasions hounds belonging to the hunt had entered the plaintiff's property and the plaintiffs alleged trespass by the defendants, their servants or agents.

Held the defendants were liable; £180 damages were awarded and an injunction for one particular area was granted.

Per Park J:

> In my judgment the law as I take it may be stated thus: where a master of staghounds takes out a pack of hounds and deliberately sets them in pursuit of a stag or hind, knowing that there is a real risk that in the pursuit hounds may enter or cross prohibited land, the master *will* be liable for trespass if he *intended* to cause hounds to enter such land, or if by his *failure* to exercise proper control over them he caused them to enter such land.

16.2.2   (2) Remaining on land after right of entry has ceased; 'holding over' by lessee is no trespass as lessor is not in present possession of the land

16.2.3   (3) Bringing anything into direct contact with land

Gregory v Piper (1820)
Plaintiff owned the wall which separated his yard from that of the defendant. In the course of a dispute about a right of way, the defendant ordered an employee to dump rubbish so as to block the way but not so as to touch

the wall; the rubbish was loose and as it dried some of it rolled against the wall.

Held the defendant was liable in trespass.

Konskier v Goodman (1928)
CA *held* leaving rubbish on roof beyond a reasonable time to be a trespass.

16.2.4   (4) Abuse of right of entry

Harrison v Duke of Rutland (1893)
Plaintiff walked up and down a road, waving a handkerchief and an umbrella; his sole intention was to interfere with the defendant's shooting.

Held (CA) that this was a trespass, he was using the highway in an *unreasonable* manner.

Hickman v Maisey (1900)
Plaintiff owned land on which racehorses were being exercised; the defendant was a racing tipster; he walked up and down road, 15 yards each way, for one-and-a-half hours, timing horses.

Held the defendant was a trespasser as he had exceeded his right of way.

Note ──
In both these cases, the party complaining of the trespass owned the land over which the road lay.
──

16.2.5   (5) Continuing trespass

Holmes v Wilson (1839)
Defendant wrongfully placed buttresses on the plaintiff's land; compensation was paid but the buttresses remained.

Held a further action for trespass lay as the buttresses had not been removed and so the trespass remained.

Compare the continuing result of a completed trespass where damages can be recovered *once* only.

16.3   Airspace
Cujus est solum, ejus est usque ad coelum et ad inferos. 'Whose is the soil, his is also that which is above it and below.'

The owner of the land owns all that lies underneath the land unless it has been leased to another or unless it belongs to the Crown. eg gold, silver, coal. The landowner can also claim the right to fill the air space above, within the limits of ordinary user.

16.3.1 The right to fill air space

Kelsen v Imperial Tobacco Co (1957)

Held, that where an advertisement belonging to the defendant projected into air space above the plaintiff's property, the plaintiff was entitled to succeed in trespass; this was not merely a nuisance and the plaintiff was entitled to a *mandatory* injunction, ie the defendant was ordered to remove it.

16.3.2 An injunction is a discretionary remedy

Woolerton v Costain (1970)

Defendant's crane swung over the plaintiff's factory 50 ft above roof level.

Held this was a trespass to the plaintiff's airspace; an injunction was granted but its operation was suspended until the defendant's building operation was concluded. Plaintiff's conduct in demanding large sums of money for permission to use the crane had been oppressive.

Charrington v Simons (1971)

The Court of Appeal *held* that it was not a proper exercise of judicial discretion to suspend the operation of an injunction – to which the plaintiff was otherwise entitled – for up to three years to enable the defendant to carry out works on the plaintiff's land; there was a strong indication that if the plaintiff did not consent to that, the injunction would be discharged. In adopting that course, trial judge had travelled *beyond* the bounds within which discretion might be judicially exercised; in effect trial judge had sought to force on the reluctant plaintiff something very like a settlement involving operations by the defendant on the plaintiff's land which must have lead to greatly increased harm to his business.

The Court of Appeal *doubted* the decision in *Woolerton v Costain* (1970).

Anchor Brewhouse Developments Ltd v Berkeley House Ltd (1987)

Defendants were developing a site and were using a tower crane in the construction work; the jib of the tower crane swung over the plaintiff's property.

Held it was a trespass to the plaintiff's air space and an injunction was granted.

Per Scott J:

It would in many respects be convenient if the court had power, in order to enable property developments to be expeditiously and economically completed, to allow, on proper commercial terms, some use to be made by the developers of the land of neighbours. But the court has no such power and ought not, in my view, to claim it indirectly by the withholding of injunctions in cases like the present ... The authorities establish, in my view, that the plaintiffs are entitled *as of course* to injunctions to restrain continuing trespass.

16.4   Aircraft

16.4.1   Civil Aviation Act 1982 s 76(1)

This provides that 'no action shall lie in respect of trespass or in respect of nuisance by reason *only* of the flight of an aircraft over any property at a height above the ground which, having regard to wind, weather and all the circumstances of the case, is *reasonable*'.

This subsection permits the use of aircraft over land belonging to another, but note that it is not an absolute right.

Section 76 (2) provides that where material loss or damage is caused to any person or property by an aircraft in flight, taking off or landing, or by any article or person falling from aircraft, damages are to be recovered *without* proof of negligence, intention or any other cause of action from the owner of the aircraft.

This subsection permits the injured person to have an *absolute* right of recovery from the owner of the aircraft provided there is no contributory negligence.

16.4.2   Right to fill air space restricted

Bernstein v Sky Views and General Ltd (1977)
Defendant took aerial photographs at a height of several hundred feet above Lord Bernstein's country house. The object of the exercise was that flattered owners would buy photographs of their property. Plaintiff claimed damages for trespass to his airspace.

Held that the defendants were not liable for trespass at common law and further that the Civil Aviation Act 1982 provided a defence.

Per Griffiths J:

> The problem is to balance the rights of the owner to enjoy the use of his land against the rights of the general public to take advantage of all that science now offers in the use of airspace. This balance is in my judgment best struck in our present society by restricting the rights of an owner in the air space above his land to such height as is necessary for the ordinary use and enjoyment of his land and the structures upon it, and declaring that above that height he has no greater rights in the airspace than any other member of the public.

Regarding the statute:

> As I read the section its protection extends to all flights provided they are at a reasonable height and comply with the statutory requirements. And I adopt this construction the more readily because sub section (2) imposes upon the owner of the aircraft a strict liability to pay damages for any material loss or damage that may be caused by his aircraft.

Q Snapper hires an aeroplane and flies over the home of Lord Snobby at a height of 250 ft; he takes aerial photographs of the Lord's home and invites

Lord Snobby to purchase prints. A week later he flies over once more at 250 ft and photographs Lady Snobby sunbathing; in his excitement Snapper drops his camera which falls into the grounds of the Snobby estate. Advise Lord and Lady Snobby.

16.5 Trespass *ab initio*

Where right of entry is given to anyone by law and he abuses that right, he shall be a trespasser ab initio.

16.5.1 There must be a positive act

The Six Carpenters' Case (1610)
Defendants refused to pay for victuals they had ordered in an inn.

Held this was not trespass *ab initio* because although there was an abuse of a right of entry conferred by *law*, refusal to pay was a mere nonfeasance, not a misfeasance.

16.5.2 Trespass *ab initio* only applies if the effect of a wrongful act is to render the entrance to premises entirely unjustified

Elias v Passmore (1934)
Police officers properly entered premises to effect a lawful arrest; whilst they were there they *improperly* seized some documents.

Held that as they were entitled to enter for the arrest, that justification *remained* and was not affected by the wrongful seizure of documents; they were trespassers *only* as to those documents.

16.5.3 Trespass *ab initio* applies when there is abuse of right of entry

Cinnamond v British Airports Authority (1980)
Unlicensed taxi drivers, who were hanging about and touting for passengers, had been prosecuted and fined.

Held (CA) that the Authority had a power and duty to turn back any person if circumstances warranted it under Airports Authority Act 1975; the taxi drivers were trespassers for they were abusing the authority given to them by law; further they were trespassers ab initio and could be turned out.

16.6 Defences

16.6.1 Licence – a consent which, without passing any interest in the property to which it relates, merely prevents the acts for which consent is given from being wrongful.

A licence may be revoked

Robson v Hallet (1967)

Three police officers went to a house; the sergeant asked to be let in and son of tenant admitted him; later tenant told sergeant to leave and he began to do so; whilst in the process of leaving he was attacked by the son; the two constables, who had been waiting outside, joined in the mêlée. DC upheld son's conviction for assault. There was an implied licence for all members of the public to go up to the door; son of the tenant had sufficient authority to admit the sergeant. The licence had been validly revoked but there had to be 'packing up' time which had not been allowed for. Further the police constables had an additional right to come to the aid of the sergeant to deal with a breach of the peace.

A licence can be made irrevocable when granted by contract for a limited time and purpose

Hurst v Picture Theatres (1915)

A cinema proprietor mistakenly believed that the plaintiff had not paid for his ticket and ejected him.

Held (CA) the plaintiff was not a trespasser during the performance for which he had a ticket. For *that* performance the licence to stay in his seat could not be revoked with the result that the defendant could not eject the customer. No amount of force could be regarded as reasonable. An injunction *could* have been obtained to prevent his expulsion and the Court of Appeal would treat the matter as if an injunction *had* been obtained. 'Equity looks on that as done which ought to be done.'

The result was that the plaintiff recovered damages for trespass to the person for the force used on him plus the price of the ticket for the breach of contract.

Q In the XYZ Cinema Cackle is enjoying a comedy film; his laughter annoys Grouch, the owner of the cinema; Grouch asks Cackle to leave, and on his refusing, ejects him from the cinema into the street. Cackle's friend Cutt is passing by and sees the eviction. Has Cackle any legal remedy?

16.6.2 Justification by law

Police and Criminal Evidence Act 1984

Section 17 a constable may enter and search premises for the purpose of arresting a person for an arrestable offence.

Section 18 there is power to enter premises *after* an arrest for an arrestable offence and to search for evidence of that offence or connected or similar offences.

When a statutory provision might be construed so as to imply power of entry, it shall be construed strictly

Morris v Beardmore (1980)

Appellant was involved in an accident; police went to his house to interview him about it; they were admitted by the son of the household. Appellant refused five requests to come down from his bedroom to discuss the accident. Through his son he requested the police to leave as they were trespassing. Police then went upstairs and asked him to give a breath sample; on his refusal he was arrested and taken to a police station where once again he refused to give a breath sample and then refused to give a blood or urine sample. Divisional Court had held that he was guilty of failure to supply samples as required by Road Traffic Act 1972 s 8(3).

The House of Lords allowed his appeal as the police had acted without authority. *Per* Lord Diplock:

> I find it quite impossible to suppose that Parliament intended that a person whose common law right to keep his home free from unauthorised intruders had been violated in this way should be bound under penal sanctions to comply with a demand which only the violation of that common law right has enabled a constable to make to him. In my opinion, in order to constitute a valid requirement the constable who makes it must be acting lawfully towards the person whom he requires to undergo a breath test at the moment that he makes the requirements. He is not acting lawfully if he is then committing the tort of trespass on that person's property for s 8(2) of that Act [which gave a constable power to require a person to provide a breath sample] gives him no authority so to do.

16.7 Remedies

16.7.1 Action at law

The plaintiff in possession can sue for interference with that possession. Trespass is actionable per se and damages may be nominal.

16.7.2 Self help

An occupier may use reasonable force to prevent a trespass continuing provided he has made a request to the trespasser to leave.

Vaughan v McKenzie (1968)

The Court of Appeal held that a bailiff cannot force his way inside to lay execution for a debt. The accused refused to let in the appellant, a County Court bailiff; he put his foot in the door to prevent her shutting it and the door was forced open; accused then hit him over the head with a milk bottle.

Held (CA) that she has *not* assaulted him in the execution of his duty, he was a *trespasser*.

Burton v Winters (1993)

Defendant built a garage which encroached by four-and-a-half inches on to the plaintiff's land; the plaintiff sought but failed to obtain a mandatory injunction to have the garage removed. She later damaged the garage and an injunction was granted against her. She disobeyed the injunction frequently and eventually was sentenced to two years imprisonment.

Held (CA) the plaintiff had no right of self help and was limited to damages; the sentence of two years was justified.

Per Lloyd LJ:

> Self help is a summary remedy, which is justified only in clear and simple cases, or in an emergency. Where a plaintiff has applied for a mandatory injunction and failed, the sole justification for a summary remedy has gone. The court has decided the very point in issue. This is so whether the complaint lies in trespass or nuisance. In the present case, the court has decided that the plaintiff is not entitled to have the wall on her side of the boundary removed. It follows that she has no right to remove it herself.

Q Domus is furious when Hibernia, a cable-laying company arrives at his house and starts to lay a cable across his front lawn. They refuse to stop their activity. What can Domus do?

16.8 Dispossession

Here the plaintiff seeks possession; the defendant in possession is not required to justify it.

16.8.1 Prior possession is sufficient title to dispossess a mere wrongdoer

Asher v Whitlock (1864)

X enclosed waste land; he devised it to his wife to be hers until she should remarry and then on that event to his daughter. Wife and daughter continued to live together on the property after X's death; wife remarried, right of possession then passed to the daughter; daughter then died.

Held that the plaintiff, daughter's heir, was entitled to possession as against the defendant, wife's second husband. Plaintiff had a good title as against all but the true owner.

16.8.2 *Jus tertii* as a defence

Carter v Barnard (1849)
Where the plaintiff is out of possession, *jus tertii* – the title of a stranger –
is a good defence; as the plaintiff is driven to assert good title, it is open to
the defendant to prove that that title is bad.

16.9 Limitation period

16.9.1 Limitation Act 1980 s 15
This provides that no action shall be brought by any person to recover land
after the expiration of *12 years* from the date on which the right of action
accrued to him. By s 17 not only the right of action is barred but the plaintiff's title is extinguished. This is the basis of possessory title; the posses-
sor for 12 years cannot himself prove good title, but he can successfully
prevent any one else claiming title.

Hayward v Challenor (1967)
Plaintiff had neglected for more than 12 years to collect from the defendant
a 'peppercorn' rent, ie a nominal rent designed to assert status of landlord
and tenant and so to prevent the limitation period from beginning to run.
When the plaintiff sought possession of his land, the defendant, the
Reverend Challoner, claimed adverse possession.
Held (CA by majority) that the plaintiff's title *had* been extinguished.

16.9.2 Possession must be adverse

Wallis v Shell (1974)
Held that mere non-user did not amount to discontinuance of possession.
Plaintiff's acts of cutting grass and grazing cattle did not prejudice the
defendant's enjoyment of land for the *purpose* for which it had been
acquired, viz development of a *garage*.

Treloar v Nute (1977)
Semble there is a burden on the true owner to establish that sufficient
special purpose.
Held that in the *absence* of evidence by the plaintiff of a special purpose,
the defendant's possession *was* adverse as against the plaintiff and the
plaintiff's title was statute barred.

17 Interference with goods

17.1 Trespass to goods

17.1.1 The tort of direct physical interference with goods which are in the possession of the plaintiff

The Winkfield (1902)
A ship was sunk by the negligent management of the defendant. Postmaster General sued for loss of mails aboard the ship.

Held he could recover although only a bailee of the mails; he would have to account, later, to the bailor. It mattered not that the plaintiff was under no liability for their loss.

17.1.2 Measure of damages

Wilson v Lombank (1963)
Plaintiff 'purchased' a car, subject to a hire-purchase agreement, from a person who had no title to it. Plaintiff sent it to a garage for repair; he was dispossessed of the car by the defendant removing it from the garage forecourt; the defendant was a hire-purchase company which had in fact no title to the car.

Held the plaintiff recovered the price he had paid for the car *plus* cost of repairs done to it subsequent to its purchase. Defendant could not plead *jus tertii* – title vested in a third party – *as against* the plaintiff who was in *possession* of the goods at the time of taking. The fact that the defendant had returned the goods to the true owner was no defence.

17.1.3 Mistake is no defence

Kirk v Gregory (1876)
X died in a state of *delirium tremens*; his servants were feasting and drinking in the house; his sister-in-law had a genuine but mistaken fear for the safety of X's jewellery; she removed the jewellery from his room and placed it in a cupboard from which it later disappeared.

Held (HL) this to be a trespass. However nominal damages only were awarded to the plaintiff, X's executor.

17.1.4 Inevitable accident is a defence

National Coal Board v Evans (1951)

In the course of excavation a servant of the defendant struck and damaged a cable belonging to the plaintiff; there was no reason to know of the existence of the cable.

Held (CA) that the plaintiff's claim failed as the *defendant* had established that what he did was an inevitable accident.

Q Compare *NCB* with *Letang v Cooper*.

17.2 Conversion

Dealing with goods in a manner inconsistent with the right of the true owner.

Fouldes v Willoughby (1841)

Defendant was manager of a Mersey ferry boat; the plaintiff came on board with two horses; there was a disagreement between the parties and in an effort to induce the plaintiff to leave the ferry, the defendant took hold of the two horses, led them ashore and let them loose.

Held that simple asportation was not enough to establish a conversion; there may have been a trespass but there was no conversion.

Per Lord Abinger CB:

> If the object, and whether rightly or wrongly entertained is immaterial, simply was to induce the plaintiff to go on shore himself, and the defendant, in furtherance of that object, did the act in question, it was not exercising over the horses any right inconsistent with, or adverse to, the rights which the plaintiff had in them ... In order to constitute a conversion, it is necessary either that the party taking the goods should intend some use to be made of them, by himself or by those for whom he acts, or that, owing to his act, the goods are destroyed or consumed, to the prejudice of the lawful owner. On instance of the latter branch of this definition, suppose in the present case, the defendant had thrown the horses into the water, whereby they were drowned, that would have amounted to an actual conversion.

17.2.1 Delivery of goods to someone other than the owner as part of a transaction affecting title is a conversion

Hollins v Fowler (1875)

Plaintiff, Fowler, sold bales of cotton to X; the cotton was not paid for; X sold on the cotton to Hollins, the defendant, who in turn sold it to Y who spun it into yarn. The cotton was now unidentifiable. Both Hollins and Fowler were innocent, but which was to bear the loss?

Held (HL) that Hollins who had bought the cotton was liable.

Per Lord Chelmsford:

Any person who, however innocently, obtains possession of the goods of a person who has been fraudulently deprived of them, and disposes of them, whether for his own benefit or that of any other person, is guilty of conversion.

Consolidated Co v Curtis (1892)

X assigned furniture to the plaintiff; X then delivered furniture to the defendant, an auctioneer, for the defendant to sell.

Held that auctioneer was liable in conversion on his selling the goods. Mistake was *no* defence.

Willis v British Car Auctions (1978)

Plaintiff hired a car to X under a hire-purchase agreement. X then tried to sell the car at the defendant's auction; car did not reach reserve price; later X was asked in the defendant's office if he would accept the highest bid and he agreed to sell the car to Y; X and Y both disappeared.

Held (CA) that the plaintiff succeeded in conversion against the defendant. Just as an auctioneer was liable when vendor had no title, when sale was 'under the hammer', so *also* was auctioneer liable when sale was made after a 'provisional bid'; in each case the auctioneer was an intermediary who brought the parties together.

The Court of Appeal was much influenced by the effect of insurance; auctioneers are insured now against such risks and charge a premium to the purchaser.

17.2.2 There is a conversion by denial of title when accompanied by some degree of control exercised over goods

Douglas Valley Finance Co v Hughes (1968)

Under a hire-purchase agreement the plaintiff hired out two lorries to X; X then 'sold' lorries to the defendant who then 'sold' lorries to Y; Y then stripped lorries of a valuable special 'A' licence; lorries were then 'resold' back up the line but this time *without* the 'A' licence; in consequence lorries lost £6,500 in value; all this time the two lorries remained in the physical possession of X.

Held the defendant was liable in conversion as, through the co-operation of X, he had been in *constructive* possession of the lorries.

17.2.3 There is a conversion when depriving a person of his goods by giving some other person a lawful title to them

Hiort v Bott (1874)

Plaintiff sent barley to the defendant by a mistake induced by their own fraudulent agent. Plaintiff then sent a 'delivery note' to the defendant which made barley deliverable to the order of consignor *or* consignee; fraudulent agent induced the defendant to endorse order to agent and to return barley to him.

Armed with delivery order, agent absconded with the barley.

Held the defendant was liable in conversion because he had actively deprived the plaintiff of his title to the barley.

Elvin Powell v Plummer Rodis (1933)

Plaintiff was induced by X to send furs to the defendant; X sent a telegram to the defendant informing him of the mistake; a confederate of X collected the furs from the defendant.

Held that the defendant had committed no conversion.

Q Distinguish *Hiort* and *Elvin Powell*.

17.2.4 Withholding possession may be sufficient

Perry v British Railways Board (1980)

There was a strike by steel workers, supported by the National Union of Railwaymen. Plaintiffs were steel stockholders who owned 500 tons of steel which was lying in British Rail depots. British Rail refused to give it up whilst admitting that the steel belonged to the plaintiffs. Defendant's motive was to avoid industrial trouble.

Held they were liable in conversion.

Per Megarry VC:

> There is a detention of the steel which is consciously adverse to the plaintiff's rights and this seems to me to be of the essence of at least one form of conversion. A denial of possession to the plaintiff does not cease to be a denial by being accompanied by a statement that the plaintiffs are entitled to the possession that is being denied to them ... For the defendants to withhold the steel from the plaintiffs is a wrongful interference with goods within the Act of 1977 unless the reason for the withholding provides a justification. I cannot see that it does. This is no brief withholding made merely in order that the defendant may verify the plaintiff's title to the steel, or for some other purpose to confirm that the delivery of the steel would be proper. This is a withholding despite the plain right of the plaintiffs to the ownership and possession of the steel, on the ground that the defendants fear unpleasant consequences if they do not deny the plaintiffs what they are entitled to.

Order for delivery up of goods was given as, in the circumstances, damages were on inadequate remedy.

17.2.5 Torts (Interference with Goods) Act 1977

Section 1 Definition of 'wrongful interference with goods'

In this Act 'wrongful interference' or 'wrongful interference with goods', means:

(a) conversion of goods (also called trover);
(b) trespass to goods;
(c) negligence so far as it results in damage to goods or to an interest in goods;

(d) subject to *section 2,* any *other* tort so far as it results in damage to goods or to an interest in goods.

Section 2 Abolition of detinue

(1) Detinue is abolished.

(2) An action lies in conversion for loss or destruction of goods which a bailee has allowed to happen in breach of his duty to bailor (that is to say lies in a case which is not otherwise conversion, but *would* have been detinue *before* detinue was abolished).

Mitchell v LB of Ealing (1978)

Plaintiff had been a squatter in the defendant's property; the defendant took possession and, by agreement, stored the plaintiff's furniture. When the plaintiff arranged to collect the furniture, the defendant mistook the place; fresh arrangements were made and in the interim the furniture was stolen.

Held the defendant was a gratuitous bailee who had been negligent in failing to return the furniture. From the moment of negligence they were the insurers of the furniture despite the fact that there had been no refusal to return. Held liable in conversion.

17.2.6 It is conversion by the defendant if his conduct will reasonably foreseeably deprive the plaintiff of his title to goods

Moorgate Mercantile v Finch (1962)

The Court of Appeal held that placing uncustomed watches in a borrowed car amounted to conversion of the car. The car, along with the watches, was seized by customs officials and forfeited under statutory powers.

Held the forfeiture was the natural and probable consequence of placing uncustomed watches in the car and so was a conversion of the *car.*

17.2.7 Basis of the plaintiff's right

At the time of the conversion, the plaintiff must be entitled to the immediate possession of the goods.

17.2.8 A finder of a lost article has legal possession

Armory v Delamirie (1721)

A chimney sweep's boy who found a jewel was held to be entitled to keep it *as against* a goldsmith's apprentice to whom it had been given for valuation.

Per Pratt CJ:

> The finder has such a property as will enable him to keep it against all but the rightful owner.

17.2.9 Where something is found on private land, owner of the land as the person entitled to immediate possession of the land is the person entitled to the thing found

South Staffordshire Water Co v Sharman (1898)

Defendant was employed to clean out a pond; he found there two rings embedded in mud.

Held that the plaintiff, owner of the land, was entitled; the right to the *control* of land carried with it the control of things in or upon it.

London Corporation v Appleyard (1963)

Defendant was employed on a demolition site; a wall safe was discovered and a large sum of money was found in a box in the safe.

Held that the leaseholder was entitled *as against* the finder. However the Corporation was entitled as the freeholder because of a term in the lease: 'Every relic or article of antiquity, rarity or value which may be found in or under any part of site shall belong to the Corporation'. The court in construing this term took a literal construction of 'value' even though it was neither antique nor of rarity; money *has* 'value'.

17.2.10 Finder is entitled when lost article is found in a public place or in a place open to the public

Bridges v Hawksworth (1851)

Bank notes were found on the floor of a shop and in that part open to the public.

Held the finder was entitled as against the shopkeeper; the goods were not under the protection of the owner of the land.

Hannah v Peel (1945)

Soldier found a brooch hidden in a house which had been requisitioned during the war.

Held he was entitled to keep the brooch although found on private land; the owner of the land had never been at liberty to enter into possession and therefore had never been in control.

17.2.11 Review of authorities by the Court of Appeal

Parker v British Airways (1982)

Held first that an occupier of *land* has rights superior to those of a finder of chattels *in* or *attached to* that land. Second, an occupier of a *building* has similar rights in respect of chattels *attached to* that building. Third, an occupier of a building has similar rights in respect of chattels *on* or *in* but *not* attached to that building *if* before the chattel is found he has manifested an intention to exercise control over the building and the things which might be on or in it. Fourth, occupier has a superior right where finder is a *trespasser*. Occupier is under an obligation to take such measures as are reasonable to ensure that lost chattels are found and to acquaint true owner of their finding.

Facts were that the plaintiff was a passenger at London Airport; he found a gold bracelet in the executive lounge of the defendant air line and handed it over to the defendant; owner of bracelet was never traced; bracelet was sold for £850 but the defendant refused to pay the proceeds to the plaintiff.

Held (CA) that on the available evidence, there was *no* sufficient manifestation of any intention to exercise control over lost property before it was found, within third principle above. As the true owner had never come forward, it was a case of 'finders keepers' *Bridges v Hawksworth* applied. Defendants were liable for conversion.

Per Donaldson LJ:

> On the evidence available there was no sufficient manifestation of any intention to exercise control over lost property before it was found such as would give the defendant a right superior to that of the plaintiff or indeed any right over the bracelet. As the true owner has never come forward, it is a case of 'finders keepers'.

17.2.12 True owner of a chattel has a title to the chattel which nobody else has

Merry v Green (1841)
A bureau had, unknown to its owner, a secret drawer containing a purse of money; the bureau was sold to another.

Held the buyer did not acquire, *as against* the seller, any lawful possession in the purse.

Moffat v Kazana (1968)
In 1951 the plaintiff bought a house; there was evidence that a tin containing money was hidden by him in that house. In 1961 the house was sold to the defendant; in 1964 the defendant found some £2,000 in a biscuit tin hidden in the chimney.

Held that the vendor of the house was entitled to the money as against the purchaser of the house; the conveyance of the house did not transfer title to the biscuit tin and therefore the plaintiff vendor was still the true owner of the tin.

Q Myopia is a holder of a second-class air ticket; he enters the passenger lounge of Ruritania Airways; he does not see a notice which says 'First class passengers only'. He does see an object on the floor which he puts in his pocket. Two weeks later, his holiday over, he goes through his pockets and finds the object – it is a valuable ring. Myopia hands it in to the Airways office. Six months later he is told the ring is unclaimed. He asks for the ring but Ruritania Airways refuse to surrender it. Advise the parties.

17.2.13 Measure of damages

The measure of damages is the value of the thing converted taken as at the time of the conversion

Chubb Cash v Crilly (1983)

Plaintiff had a hire-purchase agreement with a purchaser for a cash register; before the final instalment of the agreement was paid, purchaser permitted the defendant, a bailiff, to seize cash register on purchaser's untrue representation that the register was his. This was a conversion by the defendant of the plaintiff's goods.

Held (CA) that the measure of damages in conversion was the value of the goods at the time of conversion. This was represented by the price obtained at auction and not the unpaid instalments. Damages then were £178, not £951.

Should the value of the chattel rise after the time of conversion, then the extra value can be recovered in consequential damages

Sachs v Miklos (1948)

Plaintiff was allowed by the defendant to store furniture in the defendant's house. Plaintiff did not inform the defendant of his whereabouts; three years later the defendant twice wrote to the plaintiff requesting him to remove the furniture; no reply was received nor were letters returned; an unsuccessful attempt was made to reach the plaintiff by phone; finally the goods were sold on the defendant's orders and £15 was made on the sale. That was in 1944. In 1946 the plaintiff demanded the return of his furniture, value of which was now £115.

Held (CA) the defendant was *not* an agent of necessity and so was guilty of conversion. If the plaintiff received the letters, his damages would be £15 as his loss was caused by his own inaction; if, however, he did not receive the letters, he was entitled to the full value of £115: £15 plus £100 in *consequential* damages. Matter was remitted to trial judge for a further finding of fact.

Q Worm lends a text book to Slug who does not return it. Worm demands its return and Slug confesses he cannot find it. Worm fails his final examination and blames his failure on the loss of the book. What, if any, is the legal liability of Slug?

If the defendant has improved the goods, then he is entitled to an allowance to the extent to which the value of the goods is attributable to the improvement

Greenwood v Bennett (1972)

A car belonging to the plaintiff was stolen by X who then crashed it; X sold it to the defendant who spent £226 on repairing it.

Held (CA) that the plaintiff was entitled to the delivery of the car, then worth £400, but that the defendant was entitled to be paid the £226 he had spent on the car. The Court of Appeal pointed out that a man was not entitled to compensation for work done on the goods or property of another unless there was a contract – express or implied – to pay for it. But it was very different when he honestly believed himself to be the owner of the property and did work in that belief. The innocent 'purchaser' should be recompensed for the work done on the grounds of *unjust enrichment.*

Torts (Interference with Goods) Act 1977 s 6 is a statutory expression of *Greenwood v Bennett*

Section 6(1) If in proceedings for wrongful interference against a person (the 'improver') who has improved the goods, it is shown that the improver acted in the mistaken but honest belief that he had a good title to them, an allowance shall be made for the extent to which, at the time as at which the goods fall to be valued in assessing damages, the value of the goods is attributable to the improvement.

Q Busybody observes that there is loose guttering on the roof of Torpid's house; he takes a ladder belonging to Torpid and uses it to repair the guttering. He than rings the bell and asks Torpid for £20 for the repair. Torpid refuses to pay and Busybody, annoyed, takes away the ladder, promising to return it when he is paid. Advise Torpid.

17.2.14 Conversion and the limitation of actions

Where there are *successive* acts of conversion by the same person or different persons, in respect of the *same* property, time runs from the time of the first act – Limitation Act 1980 s 3(1). By s 3(2) after six years the plaintiff's title to the converted goods is *extinguished*. But by s 32(1) the period of limitation does not begin to run in cases of *fraud* until the plaintiff has discovered the fraud, or *could* with reasonable diligence, have discovered it.

18 Nuisance

18.1 Private nuisance – an unlawful interference with an occupiers's use or enjoyment of land or of certain incorporeal rights

18.1.1 An intent to injure or annoy is a relevant factor

Christie v Davey (1893)

Plaintiff succeeded in nuisance although he himself had been responsible for some noise which had offended the defendant; the plaintiff's noise consisted of music – his wife and daughter taught music and her son was a cellist; the defendant's noise consisted of banging trays, whistling, shrieking, knocking on partition wall, all done in a spirit of retaliation. Plaintiff was granted an injunction restraining the defendant from permitting any sounds or noises in his house so as to annoy the plaintiff or the occupiers of his house.

Per North J:

> If what has taken place had occurred between two sets of persons both perfectly innocent, I should have taken an entirely different view of the case. But I am persuaded that what was done by the defendant was done for the purpose of annoyance.

Hollywood Silver Fox Farm v Emmett (1936)

Defendant objected to the plaintiff's development of his land as a mink farm; he fired shot guns near the plaintiff's mink pens so that the animals would be disturbed while breeding. He said, 'I guarantee you will not raise a single cub'. Some vixens ate their cubs and others did not breed at all. Defendant had been annoyed by the plaintiff's conduct in erecting a notice advertising its breeding activities; the defendant feared it would put off potential purchasers of his land. Firing guns was a reasonable use of land in the country. None the less the defendant *was* liable in nuisance.

Bradford v Pickles (1895)

Plaintiff owned a waterworks and the defendant owned land from which water percolated on to the plaintiff's land, thus providing a valuable source of water. Defendant was annoyed by the plaintiff's refusal to buy his land; in retaliation he sunk a shaft on his ground which had the effect of discolouring and diminishing the plaintiff's supply.

Held (HL) that Pickle's unworthy motive in seeking to force the Corporation to purchase his land did *not* affect the rule, settled by the House of Lords in *Chasemore v Richards* (1859) that no property lies in percolating water, ie not flowing through defined channels. Plaintiff's action for nuisance failed.

Per Lord Macnaghten:

> It is the act, not the motive for the act, that must be regarded. If the act, apart from motive, gives rise merely to damage without legal injury, the motive, however reprehensible it may be, will not supply that element.

Q How can *Christie* and *Hollywood* be reconciled with *Bradford*?

18.1.2   Not every interference will be a nuisance

Bridlington Relay Ltd v Yorkshire Electricity Board (1965)
Plaintiffs operated a television relay service to provide their customers with a superior television signal; for this purpose they had a 164 ft high mast; they feared that the defendant's power line would interfere with the signal.

Held, first, that a *quia timet* injunction would not be granted; trial judge was satisfied with the defendant's assurances that every effort would be made to suppress the interference; thus the injunction sought would not add anything. 'Equity like Nature does nothing in vain.' Second, the plaintiff's use of their aerial for their business was *unusually vulnerable* to interference; they could not succeed in nuisance as they were not entitled to any greater protection than that accorded to an ordinary house holder. Third – *obiter* – that interference with a purely recreational facility, even if severe and recurrent, would not be an actionable nuisance.

Per Buckley J:

> For myself, however, I do not think that it can at present be said that the ability to receive television free from occasional, even if recurrent and severe, electrical interference is so important a part of an ordinary householder's enjoyment of his property that such interference should be regarded as a legal nuisance, particularly, perhaps, if such interference affects only one of the available alternative programmes.

Q Consider whether this *obiter* observation is true in 1995.

18.1.3   Lack of care on the defendant's part may make him liable

Andreae v Selfridge (1939)
Plaintiff kept a small hotel off Oxford Street. Defendants were rebuilding their department store in Oxford Street; as a result of their operations the hotel was covered in dust and there was noise; the hotel business slumped. Trial judge had held the defendant liable for all of the loss.

Held (CA), reversing trial judge, the defendant was not liable simply because they had caused disturbance and had used novel machinery.

Although then they could not be made responsible for all of the plaintiff's financial loss, they must be made liable for *part* of it as they had made no effort at all to minimise it.

Rapier v London Tramway Co (1893)

Defendant, acting under statutory power, set up a stable for 200 horses which were to draw trams; considerable stench resulted, amounting to a nuisance.

Held the defendants were liable, it was no defence that they had done all they could to prevent the nuisance.

Per Lindley LJ:

> At common law, if I am sued for a nuisance and the nuisance is proved, it is no defence on my part to say and to prove, that I have taken all reasonable care to prevent it.

Note ───────────────────────────────────

Reasonable care on the defendant's part is a factor in deciding whether or not a nuisance has been created by his activities. But once the court has decided that a nuisance *has* been created, then *thereafter* it is of no assistance to the defendant to plead his reasonable care.

18.1.4 Neighbourhood – some account has to be taken of the general character of neighbourhood

Sturges v Bridgman (1879)

Per Thesiger LJ:

> What would be a nuisance in Belgrave Square would not necessarily be so in Bermondsey.

There may, however, be liability for creating *more* than the *average* neighbourhood noise.

Polsue v Rushmer (1907)

Plaintiff resided by Fleet Street; the defendant had installed printing machinery next door which prevented the plaintiff from sleeping.

Held (HL) that the plaintiff was entitled to an injunction as a serious *addition* had been made to the noise of the neighbourhood.

Thompson-Schwab v Costaki (1956)

Plaintiff owned a house in a high-class residential street; the defendants were prostitutes who lived next door and who ran a brothel.

Held (CA) that an interlocutory injunction would be granted on the grounds of nuisance.

Per Lord Evershed MR:

> The plaintiffs have shown, in my opinion, a sufficient prima facie case to the effect that the activities being conducted at No 12 Chesterfield Street are not

only open, but they are notorious, and such as force themselves upon the sense of sight at least of the residents in No 13. The perambulations of the prostitutes and of their customers is something which is obvious, which is blatant, and which, as I think, the first the plaintiff has shown *prima facie* to constitute not a mere hurt of his sensibilities as a fastidious man, but so as to constitute a sensible interference with the comfortable and convenient enjoyment of his residence, where live with him his wife, son and servants.

Laws v Florinplace (1981)

Held that a sex shop in a residential area was capable of being a nuisance. Cases of nuisance were *not* confined to cases where there was some physical emanation of a damaging kind from the defendants premises. An *interlocutory* injunction was granted, demonstrating the strength of the plaintiff's case.

St Helens Smelting Co v Tipping (1865)

Plaintiff owned property near the defendant's smelting works and he complained that hedges and trees were damaged by fumes from a copper smelter.

Held (HL) the defendant were liable. It was no defence that the site of the nuisance was suitable for the operation; if no place could be found where such a business would not cause a nuisance, then it could not be carried on at all. Where alleged nuisance produced material injury to property, a plea that locality in question was devoted to such work was no defence.

Per Lord Westbury LC:

> My Lords, in matters of this description it appears to me that it is a very desirable thing to mark the difference between an action brought for a nuisance upon the ground that the alleged nuisance produces material injury to the property, and an action brought for a nuisance on the ground that the thing alleged to be a nuisance is productive of sensible personal discomfort ... But when an occupation is carried on by one person in the neighbourhood of another, and the result of that trade, or occupation, or business, is a material injury to property, then there unquestionably arises a very different consideration. I think, my Lords, that in a case of that description, the submission which is required from persons living in society to that amount of discomfort which may be necessary for the legitimate and free exercise of the trade of their neighbours, would not apply to circumstances the immediate result of which is sensible injury to the value of the property.

18.1.5 It is no defence that the plaintiff come to the nuisance

Sturges v Bridgman (1879)

Defendant had used for many years baking machinery which was near the bottom of the garden of the plaintiff, a doctor. Plaintiff was unaware of the noise made by the machinery until he built a consulting room at the foot of his garden.

Held the plaintiff succeeded in his claim for nuisance arising from noise and vibrations caused by the defendant and held he was entitled to an injunction.

Miller v Jackson (1977)

Defendants had played cricket on a small ground since 1905; in 1972 the plaintiff moved into a new house which had been built on a field adjoining cricket ground. Plaintiffs complained of cricket balls entering their property which was *below* the level of the cricket field.

Held (CA 2–1) that this *was* a nuisance but held 2–1 that an injunction would *not* be granted, on balance of conflicting interests. Plaintiffs' remedy was *limited* to damages.

The decision can be interpreted as an attempt to ameliorate a disastrous planning decision, the fact that housing was permitted to be built in an unsatisfactory location.

Kennaway v Thompson (1980)

Plaintiff lived in a house built near a lake on which the defendant organised motor boat races; the plaintiff *knew* of the races when she had the house built; subsequently the noise increased and in the Court of Appeal the defendant *admitted* liability in nuisance.

Held (CA) that an injunction *would* be granted; 'public interest' in recreation was *not* sufficient to stop the granting of an injunction. However, the injunction was limited in its terms and did not prohibit all activities of the club.

Lawton LJ cited *Shelfer v City of London Electric Lighting Co* (1895) where it was held that Lord Cairns Act 1858, in conferring upon courts of equity a jurisdiction to award damages instead of an injunction, had not altered the settled principles upon which those courts interfered by way of injunction. Held that jurisdiction under the Act should be exercised if it would be oppressive to the defendant to issue an injunction and if the injury to the plaintiff's rights was small, was capable of being estimated in money, and was one which could be adequately compensated by a money payment.

Per Lawton LJ:

The injury to the plaintiff's rights is not small, it is not capable of being estimated in terms of money save in the way the judge tried to make an estimate, namely by fixing a figure for the diminution of the value of the plaintiff's house because of the prospect of a continuing nuisance – and the figure he fixed could not be described as being small.

Q Distinguish between the two Court of Appeal decisions: *Miller* and *Kennaway*.

18.1.6 No action lies where the injury is attributable to abnormal sensitivity on the plaintiff's part

Robinson v Kilvert (1889)
Defendant manufactured paper boxes in the cellar of a building; considerable heat was required in the process; this heat damaged the plaintiff's stock of brown paper on the floor above; the heat would not have injured normal paper.
Held claim failed because the damage was caused by the paper's special sensitivity, not by the heat.
See also *Bridlington Relay Ltd v YEB* (1965) where it was held that the plaintiff's aerial was *unusually* vulnerable to interference.

Q Brazen is in the habit of playing the trombone at three in the afternoon; Febrile, his neighbour, is a night shift worker; Brazen's playing regularly wakes him up. Maddened by lack of sleep he thumps on the partition wall and blows a whistle. Has either party any legal remedy? Would it make any difference if Brazen knew that Febrile was on night shifts?

18.2 The parties

18.2.1 The plaintiff
The plaintiff must be in actual possession of land, the very person who could sue in trespass *were* the interference *direct*.

Malone v Lasky (1907)
Plaintiff was wife of tenant; whilst using the lavatory she was injured when water cistern fell on her; the defendant's electricity generator next door produced the vibrations which dislodged the cistern.
Held (CA) she had no claim in nuisance; she had no possessory right to land.

Cunard v Antifyre (1933)
Plaintiffs were tenant and his wife; guttering, which was the responsibility of the defendant, fell through the glass roof of their kitchen.
Held (1) wife could not sue in nuisance because of her lack of possessory interest; (2) *neither* of the plaintiffs could sue in nuisance because their action was base on personal injury *alone*; (3) *both* were entitled to succeed in negligence.

Khorasandjion v Bush (1993)
Plaintiff and the defendant had been friends but later fell out; the defendant began to harass the plaintiff and made persistent and unwanted telephone calls to her at her parents' and grandparents' homes.
Held (CA, 2–1) that an injunction would be granted.

Per Dillon LJ:

To my mind, it is ridiculous if in this present age the law is that the making of deliberately harassing and pestering telephone calls to a person is only action-able in the civil court if the recipient of the calls happens to have the freehold or leasehold proprietary interest in the premises in which he or she has received the calls ... Damage is, in the relevant category, a necessary ingredient in the tort of private nuisance, and I shall have to refer further to that later. So far as the harassing telephone calls are concerned, however, the inconvenience and annoyance to the occupier caused by such calls, and the interference thereby with the ordinary and reasonable use of the property are sufficient damage. The harassment is the persistent making of the unwanted telephone calls, even apart from their content; if the content is itself as here threatening and objectionable, the harassment is the greater.

Q What alternative cause of action was open to the plaintiff in *Khorasandjion*?

18.2.2 An action in nuisance may be for a continuing nuisance
Where there is a continuing actionable nuisance affecting land before and after transfer of title, the successor in title can sue in respect of it.

Master v Brent LBC (1978)
Plaintiff's house was affected by subsidence caused by roots of lime trees planted many years before by the defendant and before the plaintiff's ownership.

Held that having remedied the damage at his own expense, the plaintiff was entitled to recover damages for the cost of reinstatement.

18.3 The defendant

18.3.1 Anyone who, by a positive act, creates a nuisance, will be liable for it

Roswell v Prior (1707)
Defendant built a house which obstructed the plaintiff's ancient lights; the defendant assigned his lease and *then* was sued.

Held the defendant liable to the plaintiff in nuisance; it mattered not that, having assigned the lease, he was powerless to prevent the continu-ance of the nuisance.

18.3.2 Occupant, who is not the creator of the nuisance, is *prima facie* not liable for it

Hall v Beckenham Corporation (1949)
Model aircraft created a nuisance by noise in the defendant's public park.

Held creators of the nuisance – members of the public, who flew the aircraft – *would* have been liable if sued. But the defendant was held not liable as they had neither created the nuisance nor had they the power to prevent it.

18.3.3 Occupier will be liable for a nuisance if he does have the power to prevent it

Sedleigh-Denfield v O'Callaghan (1940)
A trespasser laid a drainage pipe upon the defendant's land; the work was defective in that a protective grating was not properly installed; the drain became blocked and as a consequence the plaintiff's land became flooded; the defendant's servant knew of the pipe but did not report it.

Held (HL) that occupiers must be presumed to have had knowledge; as they had done nothing to prevent the flooding they were liable for 'continuing' or 'adopting' the nuisance.

Per Lord Atkin:

> In the present case, however, there is as I have said sufficient proof of the knowledge of the defendants both of the cause and its probable effect. What is the legal result of the original cause being due to the act of a trespasser? In my opinion the defendants clearly continued the nuisance for they come clearly within the terms I have mentioned above they knew the danger, they were able to prevent it and they omitted to prevent it.

18.3.4 Occupier not liable if he either knew nor ought reasonably to have known of the dangerous state of affairs

Barker v Herbert (1911)
Infant plaintiff fell into the defendant's basement area through a gap in the railings; a railing had been removed by a trespasser after occupier had made his weekly inspection.

Held (CA) occupier not liable as he did not know of the defect and a weekly inspection was reasonable. There was *no* absolute duty to make the premises safe.

18.3.5 Occupier will be liable where he has employed an independent contractor to do work which necessarily results in the creation of a nuisance

Matania v National Provincial Bank (1936)
Defendant employed an independent contractor to make alterations on the first floor of a building, an operation which *necessarily* involved some

interference, by the creation of noise and dust, with the plaintiff's occupation of second floor.

Held the defendant was liable as this was a case where there was a great and obvious danger that a nuisance would be caused and which *was* caused by the failure of the independent contractor to take the necessary precautions.

18.3.6 There is general duty on occupiers in relation to hazards occurring on their land, whether natural or man-made

Goldman v Hargrave (1967)

Defendant occupied land adjacent to the plaintiff; a tree on the defendant's land was struck by lightning and caught alight, 84 ft up; midday the next day the tree was cut down; fire could then have been extinguished using water but the defendant chose to let it burn out. Three days later the wind freshened, the fire revived and spread to the plaintiff's land, causing extensive damage. JCPC held the defendant was responsible in *negligence* for this fire as the action necessary to put it out was well within his capacity and resource.

Per Lord Wilberforce

> The present case is one where liability, if it exists, rests on negligence and nothing else; whether it falls within or overlaps the boundaries of nuisance is a question of classification which need not here be resolved ... The owner of a small property where a hazard arises which threatens a neighbour with substantial interest should not have to do as much as one with larger interests of his own at stake and greater resources to protect them: if the small owner does what he can and promptly calls on his neighbour to provide additional resources, he may be held to have done his duty; he should not be liable unless it is clearly proved that he could, and reasonably in his individual circumstances should, have done more.

Leakey v National Trust (1978)

Plaintiffs owned houses next to a large mound on the defendant's land; the mound moved and encroached on the plaintiffs' land; the defendant was made aware of the problem.

Held (CA) that the defendant was liable to the plaintiffs for damages for remedial work even though the mound was a natural one and subsidence was caused by the forces of nature. Occupier is liable to owner of adjoining land for the encroachment of natural mineral material provided the defect is patent. However the defendant's obligation is what is reasonable for him as an individual to do, taking account of his means and the practicality of taking preventative measures.

Plaintiffs' claim had been properly described as a claim in nuisance, but in any event the defendant had not been prejudiced by any failure to *expressly* plead negligence.

18.3.7 Where premises abut a highway and become dangerous through disrepair, occupier will be liable for damage caused whatever the state of his knowledge

Wringe v Cohen (1940)
Gable of the defendant's shop collapsed for want of repair and damaged the plaintiff's adjoining shop. Defendant was not an occupier but an owner who had undertaken the duty to repair.

Held (CA) that he was liable *whether or not* he knew or ought to have known of the danger. It *would* have been a defence if the collapse had been caused by some secret unobservable process of nature.

18.3.8 A landlord is liable if he authorised a nuisance
Authorisation will be implied if he lets land for a purpose which will *necessarily* create a nuisance.

Metropolitan Properties Ltd v Jones (1939)
Landlord installed an electric motor in a flat so as to circulate hot water. Tenant used it in the only way it could be used and a nuisance was caused by the resultant noise.

Held landlord was liable in nuisance.

Sampson v Hodson (1981)
Plaintiff was tenant of a flat; D1 occupied a flat above the plaintiff; using the flat in a way contemplated by the landlord, a nuisance by noise was created.

Held D2 – assignee of reversion – was liable; at the time of the assignment he *knew* of the noise problem. Damages of £2,000 in lieu of an injunction were awarded against D2. Neither damages nor an injunction were awarded against D1.

Smith v Lewisham BC (1972)
Defendant council, who had acquired property next to the plaintiff, put in a homeless family; the defendant *admitted* they were not the sort of people likely to be good tenants; the defendant was *not* actuated by any improper motive.

Held (CA) that the landlord was *not* liable for nuisance caused by tenant.
Per Pennycuick VC:

> In the present case the corporation let No 25 to the Scotts as a dwelling house on conditions of tenancy which expressly prohibited the committing of a nuisance and notwithstanding that corporation knew the Scotts were likely to cause a nuisance I do not think that it is legitimate to say that the corporation impliedly authorised the nuisance.

18.3.9 Council liable if disturbance not merely likely but a necessary consequence of granting a lease

Tetley v Chitty (1986)

Defendant council granted permission to a go-kart club to develop a go-kart track on land belonging to the council. A seven year lease was granted for the express purpose of using and developing the site as a go-kart track. Plaintiffs were local rate payers and they brought an action against the council, claiming damages for noise nuisance and an injunction restraining the operation of the track.

Held council *was* liable in nuisance because the noise generated was a natural and *necessary* consequence of the operation of go-karts on the council's land and council, as landlord, had given express or at least implied consent to the nuisance on their land. Damages were an insufficient remedy and the plaintiffs were therefore entitled not only to damages but also to an injunction restraining council from permitting go-karting on the land.

Per McNeill J:

> To my mind damages would be a wholly insufficient remedy here, and the plaintiffs are entitled to an injunction. This case is unlike the *Kennaway* case in that the plaintiffs were already there and had been for some time when the nuisance began, and I have come to the conclusion that as things stand at the present there should be a permanent injunction.

Damages of £750 each were awarded to P1 and P2, £500 to P3.

18.4 Public nuisance

18.4.1 A public nuisance is an unlawful act which endangers the lives, safety, health or comfort of the public or a substantial section thereof

Attorney General v PYA Quarries Ltd (1957)

Houses near a quarry were adversely affected by dust and vibrations from quarrying operations. Defendant appealed against the grant of an injunction prohibiting a public nuisance on the basis that the nuisance was insufficiently widespread to be a public nuisance.

Held (CA) that injunction had been properly granted, there *was* a sufficiently wide impact.

Per Denning LJ:

> I decline to answer the question how many people are necessary to make up Her Majesty's subjects generally. I prefer to look to the reason of the thing and to say that a public nuisance is a nuisance which is so widespread in its range or so indiscriminate in its effect that it would not be reasonable to expect one person to take proceedings on his own responsibility to put a stop to it, but that it should

be taken on the responsibility of the community at large ... In the present case, in view of the long history of stones, vibrations and dust, I should think it incumbent on the defendants to see that nothing of the kind happens again such as to be injurious to the neighbourhood at large, even on an isolated occasion.

18.4.2 For a private civil action the plaintiff must show special and particular damage ie over and above that suffered by the public at large

Rose v Miles (1815)
Defendant blocked a creek with his barge; the plaintiff had to unload his barges and pay to have freight carried overland.
Held this was sufficient special damage to support the private claim.

Note ———————————————————————————————————
This was a case where the plaintiff was able to recover for pure economic loss resulting from obstruction.

18.4.3 Obstruction of the highway is a public nuisance

Barber v Penley (1893)
Held to be a public nuisance to cause a queue to form which caused access to the plaintiffs boarding house to be very difficult at times. Management of theatre responsible for the queue – showing 'Charlie's Aunt' – was held liable.

18.4.4 Parking on the highway can be a nuisance

Dymond v Pearce (1972)
The Court of Appeal held that onus was on the *defendant* to justify the parking of a lorry on a main road. In the circumstances, the parking of a large, lighted lorry *was* a nuisance. However the action failed as the *cause* of the collision was the plaintiff motorcyclist's negligence in not looking where he was going.

18.4.5 Liability for trees is based on knowledge

Caminer v Northern and London Investment Trust Ltd (1951)
The House of Lords held occupiers of land were not liable for the fall of an elm on to car driven by the plaintiff; the fall was caused by diseased roots.
Held there *was* a duty to inspect and *no* inspection had been made; standard of inspection was that of a reasonable and careful landowner; such an inspection would not have led to the tree being treated and so fall would not have been prevented. The failure to inspect then *did not cause* the fall and the defendants were not liable for they had no reason to suppose the tree to be dangerous.

BRS v Slater (1964)

A high lorry collided with a protruding branch; a packing case fell on to the road, causing an accident. Held the protruding branch *was* a nuisance, but the defendant was not liable because liability for nuisance depended on *knowledge*; although the presence of the branch was patent, it was not patent *as a nuisance* – no one before had ever so considered it. In those circumstances, the defendant could not be presumed to have had knowledge.

18.4.6 Highways Act 1980

Section 41 *abrogates* previous immunity for failing to keep the highway in repair.

Section 58 provides that reasonable care is a *defence*. Criteria for determining what is reasonable are:

- *character* of highway;
- *standard* of maintenance thus appropriate;
- *state of repairs* a reasonable person would expect;
- whether highway authority *knew* or could be expected to know dangerous condition;
- where it was reasonable not to have repaired before the accident, what *warning notice* was displayed.

Employment of a competent person is no defence unless it is proved that the authority gave him proper instructions and that he carried out the instructions.

Burnside v Emerson (1968)

Plaintiff was driving his car at a moderate speed in very heavy rain; D1 drove his car at a fast speed in the opposite direction; D1 hit flood water, slewed across the road and hit the plaintiff. The Court of Appeal held that D2, a highway authority, was liable. There was a failure to maintain as flooding has frequently occurred on previous occasions; D2 had *not* used all reasonable care.

Held (CA), however, it was not all the fault of D2 as D1 had driven too fast; there should be an *apportionment* of fault – two-thirds D1 and one-third D2.

18.4.7 Neighbourhood is relevant in public nuisance as in private

Gillingham BC v Medway (Chatham) Dock Co Ltd (1992)

Defendant company leased part of the old dockyard and the plaintiff council in 1983 granted planning permission to the defendant to operate a commercial port on that site. Assurances were given to the defendant by the plaintiff that they would have unrestricted access to the port. Access to the port was only possible through a residential neighbourhood; the passage of heavy goods vehicles to and from the port 24 hours a day constituted – as *conceded* by the defendant – a substantial interference with residents' enjoyment of their properties in streets through which the port traffic passed. In 1988 council brought an action in nuisance seeking a declaration that the traffic between 7 pm and 7 am constituted a public nuisance and seeking injunctions to restrain such traffic.

Held council's claim in nuisance was to be judged by reference to the character of the neighbourhood *as affected* by the planning permission granted in 1983 to use the former dockyard as a commercial port which the council had been *aware* would be used 24 hours a day. The disturbance to the residents of properties in streets through which the port traffic passed was *not* actionable.

Even if it *had* been actionable the injunctions would have been refused as a matter of *discretion* because of the assurance given by the council to the defendants, when planning permission was granted, that they would have unrestricted access to the port and that they would be consulted before any change of access was made.

Per Buckley J:

> Where planning consent is given for a development or change of use, the question of nuisance will *thereafter* fall to be decided by reference to a neighbourhood *with* that development or use and not as it was previously.

18.5 Public and private nuisance

Halsey v Esso Petroleum (1961)

Plaintiff occupied a house in a residential district. In premises adjoining the plaintiff's house, the defendant carried on an oil distribution depot. Plaintiff complained of: (1) emission of acid smuts from the defendant's chimney which damaged laundry hung out in garden and also damaged the plaintiff's car parked in road; (2) smell of nauseating nature caused by heating fuel oil; (3) noise made by boilers at night which caused house to vibrate and prevented the plaintiff from sleeping; the defendant had sound-proofed walls of boiler house, but noise remained and was not trivial; (4) noise made by tankers, enormous vehicles, which arrived at and left depot during night shift, recently introduced.

Held by Veale J:

(1)*Emission of acid smuts*

(a)under *Rylands v Fletcher* for damage done to car and laundry since damage was caused by the escape of a harmful substance; it did not matter that the plaintiff was not in possession of all of the land;

(b)　as *private* nuisance in respect of damage done to clothes – *St Helens Smelting Co v Tipping* applied;

(c)as a *public* nuisance in respect of damage done to car on public highway, there was special damage.

(2) *Smell* amounted to a private nuisance; it did not matter that there was

no injury to health. There was no right of prescription because the nause-ating smell was recent and distinct from any other smell.

(3) *Noise* of boilers and tankers when *in depot* was a *private* nuisance because noise was an inconvenience which materially interfered with ordinary physical comfort.

(4) *Noise* of tankers when *on road*:

(a) a *public* nuisance because such a concentration of vehicles was *unreason-able* use of public highway which caused special damage to the plaintiff;

(b) as a *private* nuisance, since noise was directly related to depot's opera-tion; it mattered not that subject of complaint did not emanate from the defendant's property so long as it interfered with the plaintiff's enjoy-ment of *his* property – *dictum* of Devlin J in *Southport v Esso* applied.

18.6 There can be tortious behaviour analogous to nuisance

Thomas v National Union of Mineworkers (1985)

In March 1984 the plaintiffs' branch union voted to support strike action against the mineworkers' employer, the National Coal Board. Picketing was organised by the branch union of the National Union of Mineworkers. In November the plaintiffs decided not to carry on with the strike and returned to work at their mines. They were met with the presence of 60–70 pickets outside the colliery gates each day, accompanying demonstrations and violent and abusive language. All this necessitated the plaintiffs to be brought into colliery by vehicles.

Held picketing was not actionable in tort as an assault or as obstruction; it was no assault because working miners were in vehicles and police held back pickets from the vehicles; there was no obstruction of the highway since physical entry to the colliery was not prevented. However, on the principle that any unreasonable interference with the rights of others was actionable in tort, the picketing *was* tortious as its effect was that the work-ing miners were being unreasonably harassed in the exercise of their right *to use the highway*. Since the plaintiffs had the right to use the highway to go to work and since the picketing by 60–70 pickets, in a manner which required a police presence, was intimidatory and an unreasonable harass-ment, the picketing at the colliery gates amounted to conduct which was tortious at the suit of the plaintiffs.

An injunction was granted, restraining the branch union from organis-ing members to congregate or assemble in numbers greater than six.

Per Scott J:

Nuisance is strictly concerned with, and may be regarded as confined to, activ-ity which unduly interferes with the use or enjoyment of land or easements. But there is no reason why the law should not protect on a similar basis the enjoyment of other rights. All citizens have the right to use the public highway. Suppose an individual were persistently to follow another on a public highway, making rude gestures or remarks in order to annoy or vex. If continuance of such conduct were threatened no one can doubt but that a civil court would, at the suit of the victim, restrain by an injunction continuance of the conduct. The tort might be described as a species of private nuisance, namely as an unreasonable interference with the victims right to use the highway but the label for the tort does not, in my view, matter.

Q In a residential area a contraceptive manufacturer, Latex, is given planning permission to store and distribute contraceptives. Neighbours complain of the noise and smell of the traffic generated. Further they complain of the nature of the trade. Some assemble at the warehouse gates to protest. Banners and fists are shaken at the drivers. Several drivers complain they are followed by residents' cars. Consider the legal position.

19 The rule in *Rylands v Fletcher*

19.1 'The person who for his own purposes brings on his lands and collects and keeps there anything likely to do mischief if it escapes, must keep it in at his peril, and if he does not do so is *prima facie* answerable for all the damage which is the natural consequence of its escape'
per **Blackburn J** *Fletcher v Rylands* **(1866)**

Facts of that case were that the defendant constructed a reservoir upon his land in order to supply water to his mill; upon the site chosen for this purpose there was a disused and filled-up shaft of an old coal mine, the passages of which communicated with the adjoining mine of the the plaintiff; through the negligence of the independent contractor employed by the defendant, this fact was not discovered and the danger caused by it was not guarded against. When the reservoir was filled the water escaped down the shaft and thence into the plaintiff's mine which it flooded.

Held the defendant was liable and the House of Lords dismissed his appeal.
Per Lord Cranworth:

My Lords, I concur with my noble and learned friend in thinking that the rule of law was correctly stated by Mr Justice Blackburn is delivering the opinion of the Exchequer Chamber. If a person brings, or accumulates, on his land anything which, if it should escape, may cause damage to his neighbour, he does so at his peril. If it does escape, and cause damage, he is responsible, however careful he may have been, and whatever precautions he may have taken to prevent the damage.

19.2 Limits of the rule

19.2.1 Liability will only be imposed if there is an 'escape' of the object from land in the defendant's occupation or control

Read v Lyons (1946)
Plaintiff was an inspector of munitions; in the course of her employment she was injured on the defendant's premises by the explosion of a shell; there was *no* allegation of negligence.

Held (HL) she could not succeed under the Rule because her injury was caused and suffered *on* the defendant's property; there was therefore no 'escape' and the defendant was not liable.

Per Viscount Simon:

'Escape' for the purpose of applying the proposition in *Rylands v Fletcher* means escape from a place which the defendant has occupation of, or control over, to a place which is outside his occupation or control. Blackburn J several times refers to the defendant's duty of 'keeping a thing in' at the defendant's peril and by 'keeping in' he means, not preventing an explosive substance from exploding, but preventing a thing which may inflict mischief from escaping from the area which the defendant occupies or controls.

19.2.2 The House of Lords in *Rylands v Fletcher* held that strict liability was only to be imposed in the case of 'non-natural' use of land

Per Lord Cairns LC:

If the defendants, not stopping at the natural use of their close, had desired to use it for any purpose which I may term *a non-natural use*, for the purpose of introducing into the close that which in its natural condition was not in or upon it.

Cf *Per* Blackburn J:

And it seems but reasonable and just that the neighbour, who has brought something on his own property *which was not naturally there*, harmless to others so long as it is confined to his own property, but which he knows to be mischievous if it gets on his neighbours', should be obliged to make good the damage which ensues if he does not succeed in confining it to his own property.

19.2.3 Probably all that was intended by Lord Cairns was to draw the distinction between natural and artificial accumulation

Smith v Kenrick (1849)

Defendant's coal mine contained a subterranean lake, an accumulation of rain water bounded by a bar of coal; it was obvious that if that bar of coal were mined, the water would be released and would gravitate into the plaintiff's mines; nevertheless the defendant mined the coal.

Held the defendant *not* liable.

Whalley v Lancashire and Yorkshire Railway (1884)

An unprecedented storm flooded the drains bordering on the defendant's railway embankment; in consequence a large quantity of water was dammed up against the embankment; the level of the water rose, endangering the embankment; the defendant then pierced embankment to relieve the pressure, and the water so released flooded on to the plaintiff's land.

Held the defendant *was* liable.

19.2.4 Natural and non-natural use

Rainham Chemical Works v Belvedere Fish Guano (1921)
Held (HL) that it was a non-natural user of land to make munitions on it during First World War – but this was assumed without argument.

Read v Lyons (1946)
The House of Lords were prepared to say that the manufacture of munitions *was* a natural user, certainly if it were done at the government's request, in time of war, for the purpose of defeating the enemy.

British Celanese v Hunt (1969)
On a preliminary issue, it was held that storing metal foil for the purpose of manufacturing electrical components *was* a natural user of a trading estate site because the use of such premises for storing such material did not by itself create *special risks*. On the facts however there was potential liability in *negligence* for economic loss; the metal foil had been carelessly stored and some blew away; the defendants were aware from previous experience that this was likely to happen; the escaped foil landed on an electricity sub-station and shorted out the plaintiff's electricity supply.
Per Lawton J:

> The defendants are alleged to occupy premises on a trading estate. Such estates are planned and laid out for the purpose of accommodating manufacturers. The defendants are manufacturers. It follows that they are using this site for the very purpose for which sites were made available on the estate. The use of the site for manufacturing would be an ordinary one; the use of the site for any other purpose would be unusual.

> Does the particular kind of manufacturing which is done in the defendant's factory constitute, in Lord Moulton's words, 'some special use bringing with it increased danger to others'? The manufacturing of electrical and electronic components in the year of 1964, which is the material date, cannot be adjudged to be a special use nor can the bringing and storing on the premises of metal foil be a special use in itself. The way the metal foil was stored may have been a negligent one; but the use of the premises for storing such foil did not by itself create special risks.

19.2.5 People may be considered as potential *Rylands v Fletcher* objects

Attorney General v Corke (1933)
Defendant allowed 200–300 caravan dwellers to place their caravans on his disused brickfield, near Bromley in Kent. Some of them wandered off and defecated on neighbouring land.
Held Rylands v Fletcher applied.

Per Bennett J:

It is, of course, not unlawful for a person to grant licences to caravan dwellers to place caravans on his land. But it seems to me that, in bringing on to his land, for his own profit, a number of people who dwell in caravans, the defendant has put his land to an abnormal use. Persons whose homes are in caravans, moving about from place to place, have habits of life many of which are offensive to those who have fixed homes, and when collected together in large numbers, on a comparatively small parcel of land, such persons would be expected by reasonable people to do the kind of things which have been complained of in this action.

Q Was this case correctly decided?

Q Agricola is a farmer; he rents a field to Pollux who then sets up a commune for his friends; they roam the neighbourhood, fouling adjoining fields and disturbing livestock. What remedy, if any, have the neighbours?

19.3 Defences

19.3.1 *Volenti non fit injuria*

Peters v Prince of Wales Theatre (1942)
Tenant of shop was held to have *consented* to the presence of a sprinkler system in the theatre when he took the lease; consequently his landlords, proprietors of the adjoining theatre, were held not liable, in the absence of negligence on their part, when pipes froze during a frost and in consequence tenant's shop was flooded.

Thomas v Lewis (1937)
Plaintiff and the defendant occupied adjoining lands; the plaintiff was a farmer and the defendant owned a quarry; the defendant granted the plaintiff grazing rights over part of the defendant's land; the plaintiff complained of damage *both* to his *farm* and to the land granted. Held he succeeded in respect of the *farm* but not in respect of the land granted, for the grant of grazing rights must be taken to have implied a right of the grantor – the defendant – to continue to cast stones on the land as before.

19.3.2 Default of the plaintiff
Fletcher v Rylands (1866)
Per Blackburn J:

He can excuse himself by showing that the escape was owing to the plaintiff's default.

Ponting v Noakes (1894)
Plaintiff's horse reached over the defendant's boundary and nibbled a poisonous tree situated there.

Held the defendant was not liable for the death of the horse; first because there had been no 'escape' and secondly the damage was due to the horse's *own* intrusion.

19.3.3 Act of a stranger

Rickards v Lothian (1913)

Defendant had sublet office floor to the plaintiff; some unknown person had blocked waste-pipe of a wash-basin on the floor above, which was in the defendant's control; the plaintiff's stock in trade was damaged by the overflow.

Held (JCPC) that the defendant was not liable since damage was due to the act of a stranger which the defendant could not reasonably have prevented.

Per Lord Moulton:

A defendant cannot, in their Lordships' opinion, be properly said to have caused or allowed the water to escape if the malicious act of a third person was the real cause of its escaping without any fault on the part of the defendant ... Their Lordships are of the opinion that a defendant is not liable on the principle of *Rylands v Fletcher* for damage caused by the wrongful act of third persons.

Further held that the use of the premises was *not* non-natural.

Per Lord Moulton:

The provision of a proper supply of water to the various parts of the house is not only reasonable, but has become, in accordance with modern sanitary views, an almost necessary feature of town life. It is recognised as being so desirable in the interests of the community that in some form or other it is usually made obligatory in civilised countries. Such a supply cannot be installed without causing some concurrent danger of leakage or overflow. It would be unreasonable for the law to regard those who install or maintain such a system of supply as doing so at their own peril, with an absolute liability for any damage resulting from its presence even when there has been no negligence. It would still be more unreasonable if, as the respondent contends, such liability were to be held to extend to the consequences of malicious acts on the part of third persons.

Perry v Kendricks Transport (1956)

Defendant owned a garage and car park; in the park was a motor coach, the petrol tank of which had been emptied and the cap replaced; there was regular inspection of both car park and of vehicle. Plaintiff crossed adjacent waste-land when a boy, standing by the coach, threw a lighted match into the tank, the cap of which had been removed; the plaintiff was injured in the resultant explosion.

Held (CA) that a coach with petrol vapour in the tank was a *Rylands v Fletcher* object and the plaintiff *could* sue for his personal injuries under the Rule; however the explosion was the result of the acts of a stranger over whom the defendant had no control; *Rickards v Lothian* applied and claim failed.

Per Jenkins LJ:

If the facts are such as to show that the dangerous thing was left by the defendants in such a condition that it was a reasonable and probable consequence of their action, which they ought to have foreseen, that children might meddle with the dangerous thing and cause it to escape, then the defendants could not maintain for the purposes of *Rylands v Fletcher* that the mischievous acts of the children constituted the acts of strangers. But then claim merges in to a claim in negligence and it would no longer be necessary to rely on *Rylands v Fletcher* at all.

North Western Utilities Ltd v London Guarantee (1936)
Plaintiff owned an hotel in city; city authorities removed soil from beneath the defendant's gas pipes whilst constructing a sewer; deprived of support, a gas pipe broke, gas escaped and caught fire, destroying the plaintiff's hotel.

Held (JCPC) the defendant *liable*. Defendant *knew* of the excavations beneath pipe but had done nothing to prevent the breakage which they could have foreseen together, with its consequences.

Q Ferrous collects scrap metal in his yard. Steel, a well known local thief, enters the yard and takes an army shell amidst the scrap. He runs off with the shell, but whilst crossing the premises of Copper, he trips over and drops the shell. The resultant explosion destroys Copper's house. Consider legal liability.

19.3.4 Act of God
A process of nature, not due to any act of man, in circumstances which no human foresight could provide against and of which human prudence is not bound to recognise the possibility.

Nichols v Marsland (1876)
Defendant possessed artificial pools formed by damming a natural stream; dam was well constructed and in good condition; a storm – the heaviest within human memory – caused water to overflow and the rush of water carried away bridges belonging to the plaintiff.

Held (CA) that the defendant was not liable for an extraordinary act of nature which he could not reasonably have anticipated.

> Note
> This is the only recorded case where this defence has been successful.

Greenock Corporation v Caledonian Railway (1917)
Corporation diverted a stream to make a children's paddling pool; owing to rainfall of extraordinary violence, the stream overflowed at the pool and flooded property of railway company; if stream had been in its original state, flood would not have occurred.

Held (HL) that this was not an Act of God.

(Can anyone say that such rainfall was unprecedented in Scotland?)

19.3.5 Statutory authority

This is a defence even under *Rylands v Fletcher* but if there be negligence the protection ceases – *Geddis v Ban Reservoir* (1875).

Dunne v NW Gas Board (1963)

Plaintiff was blown off her bicycle by a gas explosion; gas had escaped from a gas main belonging to the defendant; gas travelled along a sewer and somehow became ignited; gas main had broken because of a withdrawal of support, caused by the bursting of a water main belonging to Liverpool Corporation, D2. The Court of Appeal held *neither* of DD liable.

D1 was not liable, either under *Rylands v Fletcher* or in nuisance because it had done, without negligence, what the Gas Act 1948 imposed on them. D2 was not liable under *Rylands v Fletcher*. *Geddis v Bann Reservoir* applied where the House of Lords held that a statutory undertaker is immune where statutory powers are exercised without negligence, ie with all reasonable regard and care for the interests of other persons. D2 was not liable in nuisance because its statutory power has *no* 'nuisance clause', ie a clause which rendered statutory undertaker prima facie liable in nuisance.

The Court of Appeal in *Dunne v NW Gas Board* remarked that it scarcely seemed accurate to hold that a nationalised industry collected and distributed gas for its 'own purposes'. This approach was followed in:

Pearson v NW Gas Board (1968)

Plaintiff was injured in a gas explosion; her husband was killed and their home destroyed. They themselves were not supplied with gas; the escape of gas was due to a fractured gas main, caused by earth movements which were a result of the severe frost experienced in the winter of 1963. Expert evidence for the defendant was to the effect that no reasonable steps were open to safeguard the public from this hazard. Plaintiff's counsel *conceded* (regrettably) that *Rylands v Fletcher* was inapplicable.

Held – assuming *res ipsa loquitur* applied – the expert evidence rebutted the presumption of negligence. Accordingly, the plaintiff's claim failed.

Pearson is a remarkable and lamentable example of the failure of the law of tort to compensate an innocent and blameless plaintiff.

19.4 Remoteness of damage

19.4.1 Test for remoteness of damage is the same as in nuisance and negligence – reasonable foreseeability

Cambridge Water Co v Eastern Countries Leather (1994)
Defendants operated a tannery at Sawston, near Cambridge. As a part of the tannery process the defendant used a chemical perchloroethene (PCE). Up to 1976 it was delivered to their premises in drums; in the process of transferring the chemical there was a regular spillage of small quantities which over the years amounted to 1,000 gallons. PCE soaked through the concrete floor and slowly dissolved into percolating ground water. The contaminated water affected the plaintiff's bore hole over a mile away; it was not foreseeable that such repeated spillage of small quantities of PCE would lead to any environmental hazard for it was likely that there would be evaporation rather than any seepage through concrete. Water was not declared unwholesome until 1982. Plaintiff had to close bore hole and drill a new one at a cost of nearly a million pounds.

Held (HL) that the defendant's operation was a *Rylands v Fletcher* activity as a non-natural use of land.

Per Lord Goff:

> The mere fact that the use is common in the tanning industry cannot, in my opinion, be enough to bring the use within the exception, nor the fact that Sawston contains a small industrial community which is worthy of encouragement and support. Indeed I feel bound to say that the storage of substantial quantities of chemicals on industrial premises should be regarded as an almost classic case of non-natural use; and I find it very difficult to think that it should be thought objectionable to impose strict liability for damage caused in the event of their escape.

Second, the House of Lords *held*, allowing appeal the defendants were *not* liable. The damage was *too remote* as it was not reasonably foreseeable.

Per Lord Goff:

> Professor Newark has convincingly shown that the rule in *Rylands v Fletcher* was essentially concerned with an extension of the law of nuisance to cases of isolated escape. Accordingly since, following the observations of Lord Reid when delivering the advice of the Privy Council in *The Wagon Mound (No 2)* the recovery of damages in private nuisance depends on foreseeability by the defendant of the relevant type of damage, it would appear logical to extend the same requirement to liability under the rule in *Rylands v Fletcher* ... It appears to me to be appropriate now to take the view that foreseeability of damage of the relevant type should be regarded as a prerequisite of liability in damages under the rule ... In the result, since those responsible at ECL could not at the relevant time reasonably have foreseen that the damage in question might occur, the claim of CWC for damages under the rule in *Rylands v Fletcher* must fail.

20 Fire

20.1 Fires Prevention (Metropolis) Act 1774

20.1.1 Section 86 provides that those in whose premises fire accidentally begins will *not* be liable for the escape of fire

Filliter v Phipppard (1847)

Defendant lit a fire on his land which spread to the plaintiff's fields. Defendant was held liable, the court pointing out that 'accidentally begin' means a fire produced by mere chance or incapable of being traced to any cause.

Held that the Act, despite its title, was *not* confined to London. Fires due to negligence were *still* a source of liability.

Collingwood v Home and Colonial Stores (1936)

A fire started in defendant's premises due to some defect in the electric wiring; the fire spread to the plaintiff's premises.

Held (CA) that the defendant was protected by the statute as the plaintiff had failed to establish negligence. Further *Rylands v Fletcher* did not apply as domestic use of electricity was a natural user of land.

20.2 Even if a fire arises by accident, occupier will be liable if he negligently permits it to spread

Musgrove v Pandelis (1919)

Plaintiff's property was destroyed by a fire which had started in the carburettor of defendant's car whilst defendant's servant was cleaning it; fire had started by accident but the servant was negligent because he had stupidly neglected to turn off the petrol tap which at that time was fitted to all cars; this simple action would have stopped the initial fire.

Held (CA) defendant liable. Further it was held that a car was a *Rylands v Fletcher* object – *sed quaere*.

Goldman v Hargrave (1967)

A tree on defendant's land was struck by lighting and caught alight; midday the next day the tree was felled and the fire should have been put out by using water but defendant chose to let it burn out; three days later wind freshened, fire revived and spread to the plaintiff's land, causing extensive damage.

Held defendant *was* responsible, as action necessary to put it out was well within his resources. Section 86 was no defence as the relevant fire – the one three days later – was *not* accidental. JCPC pointed out that there was a general duty on occupiers in relation to hazards occurring on their land, whether natural *or* man-made.

20.3 Even if fire is lit intentionally but spread without negligence, there is no liability

Sochaki v Sas (1947)

Fire lit by lodger spread from an ordinary domestic grate and damaged the house. Held there was no liability as there was no evidence of negligence. It was not a case of *res ipsa loquitur* for 'everyone knows fires occur through accidents which happen without negligence on anybody's part' *per* Goddard LCJ.

20.4 The only circumstance when the occupier is not liable for negligence is when it is the negligence of a stranger

Balfour v Barty King (1957)

Defendant occupied part of a house and the plaintiff occupied adjoining part; defendant invited workmen, as independent contractors to thaw frozen water pipes in loft; workmen proceeded to do this by applying a blow lamp to the pipes; some lagging caught fire and the fire spread to the plaintiff's premises.

Held (CA) that the defendant was liable; fire was not 'accidental' within the meaning of s 86; it was not the act of a stranger because the independent contractors had been *chosen* by defendant, *invited* to do the work and could have been *ordered to leave* at any moment.

20.5 Liability is based on occupation

Sturge v Hackett (1962)

Defendant was tenant of first floor flat; whilst trying to smoke out a bird's nest in roof he used a paraffin soaked rag on the end of a stick; he set fire to the roof and burned down the house. Negligence was *admitted*. Defendant had an insurance policy insuring him as *occupier* – maximum cover £100,000; it also insured him for *personal* liability – maximum cover £10,000. Actual damage was £16,000. Held by the Court of Appeal that although *Musgrove v Pandelis* and *Balfour v Barty-King* could have been decided on the basis of vicarious liability, the actual *ratio decidendi* was that liability was based on occupation and the Court of Appeal was bound by it. Defendant then was covered by his insurance for occupier's liability, ie up to £100,000.

20.6 There may be more than one occupier

Emmanuel v GLC (1971)

Plaintiff was a furniture maker and D1 owned an adjoining site on which there were two 'pre-fabs'; under statutory provisions D1 asked Ministry of Housing to remove the pre-fabs. D1 kept control over them, they had a foreman who kept the keys. Ministry of Housing asked Ministry of Works to remove the structures; Ministry of Works then sold them to D2, a contractor. The contract contained a clause, forbidding the burning of rubbish; it *was* burned and fire spread to the plaintiff's premises.

Held (CA) that D1 were *occupiers* of the site as they had sufficient degree of control; *possibly* Ministries of Housing and Works were also occupiers – remarkably they were not parties to the litigation. Contractors D2, *another* occupier, were not 'strangers' to D1; they were present with the leave and knowledge of D1 who could reasonably have anticipated that D2 might start a fire, for it was their regular practice to burn rubbish. D1 was therefore liable to the plaintiff.

20.7 Liability may be imposed on a principle analogous to *Rylands v Fletcher*

Mason v Levy Auto (1967)

Defendant, whose property adjoined the plaintiff's, stored in his yard high stacks of machinery covered in grease, oil and waxed paper; this was a serious fire risk; a fire did ensue and damaged the plaintiff's property.

Held, where the protection of s 86 was invoked, it was for the *plaintiff* to show negligence on the part of the defendant; the plaintiff had *failed* to do that. However he succeeded on a principle *analogous* to *Rylands v Fletcher*, analogous because it was not the thing brought on to the land which escaped. McKenna J accepted that the same rule of strict liability applied where the non-natural thing caught fire and it was the fire that escaped from the land.

Defendant is liable if: (a) he brought on to his land things *likely* to catch fire and kept them there in such conditions that, if they did ignite, the fire would be likely to *spread* to the plaintiff's land; (b) he did so in the course of some *non-natural* use; (c) the things ignited and the fire spread.

On *that* principle the plaintiff succeeded as use *was* non-natural because of: (1) quantities of combustible material; (2) manner of storage; (3) character of neighbourhood.

Q Lucifer, a lodger, lights a coal fire in his sitting room; he then leaves the room to make his tea; a spark jumps from the grate and sets fire to the room. Fire spreads to the neighbouring house owned by Miss Jones. Advise Rigsby, the landlord and Miss Jones.

20.8   Statutory liability

20.8.1   Nuclear Installations Act 1965

Section 7 Duty of licensees of licensed site:

(1) Where a nuclear site licence has been granted in respect of any site, it shall be the duty of the licensee to secure that (a) no such occurrence involving nuclear matter ... causes injury to any person or damage to any property of any person other than the licensee.

Merlin v British Nuclear Fuels (1990)

Plaintiffs owned a house six miles south of the defendant's plant at Sellafield. Tests on dust from the house showed high levels of radio active contamination; it was *admitted* that the contamination originated from the defendant's plant. Plaintiffs put their house on the market for £65,000 but it was eventually sold at auction for £35,000.

Held the defendants were not liable. First, economic loss was *not* covered by the statute. Secondly, that injury to the person did *not* include the risk of injury in the *future*. There was no other loss and accordingly the claim failed.

Per Gatehouse J:

> Personal injury or damage to property' is a familiar enough phrase and in my judgment it means, as it does in other contexts, physical (or mental) injury or physical damage to tangible property ... I reject the argument that contamination of the plaintiffs' house *per se* amounts to damage to their property. All that such contamination as was admitted in this case amounts to is some increased risk to the health of its occupants. The Act of 1965 compensates for proved personal injury, not the risk of future personal injury.

21 Defences

21.1 *Volenti non fit injuria*

No action in tort will lie in respect of a risk knowingly and voluntarily assumed.

21.2 The maxim applies to accidental harm in circumstances which would otherwise be negligent

Cutler v United Dairies (1933)

Plaintiff went into a field in which he saw a restive horse which a van driver was attempting to pacify; the driver shouted, 'Help! Help!' whereupon the plaintiff went to hold the horse which suddenly reared, injuring him.

Held (CA) that the defendant was not liable, the plaintiff had *assumed* the risk; cause of the accident was not the negligence, if any, of the defendant employing such a horse but a *novus actus interveniens*, the plaintiff's attempt to hold a horse, the risk of which he knew.

21.3 The maxim is not *scienti non fit injuria*

Smith v Baker (1891)

Plaintiff was employed in a quarry to drill stones in a cutting over which large stones were jibbed in the sling of a crane. He had previously reported his view that this practice was dangerous. Due to the negligence of the defendants, he was injured by a falling stone.

Held (HL) defence of *volenti non fit injuria* failed.

Per Lord Halsbury LC:

> It appears to me that the proposition upon which the defendants must rely must be a far wider one than is involved in the maxim *volenti non fit injuria*. I think they must go to the extent of saying that whenever a person knows there is a risk of injury to himself, he debars himself from any right of complaint if an injury should happen to him in doing anything which involves that risk ... and if applicable to the extent that is now insisted on, no person ever ought to have been awarded damages for being run over in London streets; for no one (at all events some years ago before the admirable police regulations of later years) could have crossed London streets without knowing that there was a risk of being run over.

Bowater v Rowley Regis Corporation (1944)

Plaintiff *knew* that a horse was given to bolting.

Held (CA) he was entitled to recover damages for his injuries, inflicted when the horse in fact did bolt; he had been ordered to use the horse, despite his protests as to its unsuitability. Defendant was not entitled to make him elect between losing his job and risking injury.

21.4 The consent must have been freely given

R v Williams (1923)

Held consent was no defence to a charge of rape when the consent was given in the fraudulently induced belief – by the victim's singing teacher – that sexual intercourse would improve her voice.

Freeman v Home Office (1984)

The Court of Appeal *held* that where, in a prison setting, a doctor had the power to influence a prisoner's situation and prospects, a court must be alive to the risk that what might appear, on the face of it, to be a real consent, was not in fact so. Nevertheless a prisoner *can* give effective consent to treatment by a prison doctor. The matter was one of fact. Trial judge had found as a fact that the plaintiff prisoner had consented to the injection of drugs. Appeal by the plaintiff dismissed.

Latter v Braddell (1881)

Plaintiff's mistress believed her to be pregnant and insisted that she be examined by a doctor; after some protest the plaintiff, a house maid, submitted to examination by the doctor. The Court of Appeal *rejected* the plaintiff's appeal from the withdrawal from the jury of the case against her employers and the finding of the jury in favour of the doctor.

Held (CA) this was no assault, either by the mistress or by the doctor. Consent was deemed to have been freely given even though it was given reluctantly or under the mistaken belief that the defendant was entitled to act as she did.

Q Consider whether *Latter* was correctly decided.

21.5 There are limits to the operation of the consent

Lane v Holloway (1967)

After an altercation, the plaintiff aged 64, struck the defendant, aged 23, on the shoulder; the defendant then struck the plaintiff a savage blow in the eye, causing injury which necessitated 19 stitches.

Held that even if the fight started out by being unlawful, one party *could* sue the other for damages for an injury if it were inflicted by a savage blow out of all proportion to the occasion. Plaintiff had *not* taken on himself the risk of such an injury.

21.6 *Volenti* is no defence to a breach of the statutory duty

Wheeler v New Merton Board Mills (1933)

The Court of Appeal *held* it to be no defence to a breach of statutory duty that the plaintiff, a workman, had in fact consented to work on unguarded dangerous machinery. Clearly it is a matter of public policy that a private agreement should not set aside the will of Parliament.

However where the employer is not in breach of any of his statutory duties, then volenti may be a defence.

ICI v Shatwell (1964)

Two employees *jointly* decided to disregard safety precautions in the face of express prohibition by both employer and of statutory regulations.

Held (HL) that the defendant *was* entitled to plead *volenti* to an action by one of them for the negligence of the other, for whom the defendant was *vicariously* responsible. Lord Pearce pointed out that this principle should be limited to cases where the breach of statutory duty was *not* caused by the failure of some person of superior rank to the plaintiff and whose commands the plaintiff was bound to obey.

21.7 It must be shown that the plaintiff had a choice

Burnett v British Waterways Board (1973)

Plaintiff was an employee on a barge sent to the defendants' dock; at the entrance to the dock there was a notice stating that barge workers entering dock did so as their own risk; a rope broke and injured the plaintiff.

Held (CA) that on the facts the plaintiff had *no* free choice – he had to do the job he was sent to do and was not voluntarily incurring the risk of negligence on the part of the defendant. *Volenti* was only available when the plaintiff freely and voluntarily, with full knowledge of the nature and extent of the risk, impliedly agreed to incur it and *to waive any claim for injury.* No such agreement could possibly have been implied in that case.

21.8 Special situations

21.8.1 Medical treatment

Family Law Reform Act 1969

By s 8(1) the consent of a minor, who has attained the age of 16 years, to any surgical, medical, or dental treatment which, in the absence of consent, *would* constitute a trespass to the person, shall be as effective as it would be if he *were* of full age.

By s 8(3) nothing in the section is to be construed as making ineffective any consent which would have been effective if that section had not been enacted.

Thus the subsection recognises that a minor has at *common law* the capacity to consent.

Gillick v West Norfolk AHA (1985)

The House of Lords *held* 3–2 that a girl under 16 did not merely, by reason of age, lack legal capacity to consent to contraceptive advice and treatment by a doctor. There was *no* rule of absolute parental authority until a fixed age – parental authority 'dwindled' with the years. Doctor then had a *discretion* to give contraceptive advice and treatment to a girl under 16 without her parents' consent provided the girl had reached an age where she had sufficient understanding and intelligence to understand fully what was proposed; *that* was a question of *fact* in each case.

Consent may be supplied by the court for treatment given

Re S (1992)

Health authority applied for declaration to authorise surgeon and staff of hospital to carry out an emergency caesarean section operation on Mrs S who was in labour. She refused consent on religious grounds. It was an emergency situation. Application came on at 1.30 pm and hearing commenced just before 2.0 pm. Declaration was made at 2.18 pm. Authorisation was granted by Sir Stephen Brown P.

Held such on operation was vital to protect the life of the unborn child and in its inherent jurisdiction court would grant the declaration sought.

Re T (1992)

T was injured in a car accident when she was 34 weeks pregnant and was admitted to hospital. T went into labour and it was decided that delivery should be by Caesarean section; she told medical staff that she did not want a blood transfusion; she herself was not a Jehovah's Witness but her mother was. After an emergency Caesarean operation her condition deteriorated and she was transferred to an intensive care unit.

Held (CA) that on the facts doctors had been justified in disregarding T's instructions. Administering a blood transfusion was a matter of necessity. Evidence showed that T had not been fit to make a genuine decision because of her medical condition – in pain and under the influence of drugs. Further she was subject to the undue influence of her mother.

Per Lord Donaldson MR:

> The law requires that an adult patient who is mentally and physically capable of exercising a choice must consent if medical treatment to him is to be lawful, although the consent need not be in writing and may sometimes be inferred from the patient's conduct in the context of surrounding circumstances. Treating him without his consent or despite a refusal of consent will constitute

the civil wrong of trespass to the person and may constitute a crime. If, however, the patient has made no choice and, when the need for treatment arises, is in no position to make one, eg the classic emergency situation with an unconscious patient, the practitioner can lawfully treat the patient in accordance with his clinical judgment of what is in the patient's best interest.

F v West Berkshire Health Authority (1989)

Plaintiff was a woman of 36; she suffered from serious mental disability. Since the age of 14 she had been a voluntary in-patient at a mental hospital controlled by the defendant. She had formed a sexual relationship with a male patient. It would have been disastrous for her to become pregnant. Her mother sought a declaration that the absence of patient's consent would not make her sterilisation unlawful.

Held (HL) that the judge had been right to grant the declaration sought and the appeal by the Official Solicitor was dismissed.

Per Lord Brandon:

A doctor can lawfully operate on, or give other treatment to adult patients who are incapable, for one reason or another, of consenting to his doing so, *provided* that the operation or other treatment concerned, is in the best interests of such patients. The operation or other treatment *will* be in their best interests *if*, but only if, it is carried out in order either to save their lives or to ensure improvement or to prevent deterioration in their physical or mental health.

Consent may be supplied by the court for treatment to be withheld

Airedale NHS Trust v Bland (1993)

Patient in care of health authority had been in a persistent vegetative state for three-and-a-half years after suffering a severe crushed chest injury sustained in the Hillsborough football disaster. Doctors were unanimous that there was no hope whatsoever of recovery or improvement. Health authority sought declarations that it and responsible physicians could lawfully discontinue all life sustaining treatment.

Held (HL) that a doctor who had in his care a patient who was incapable of deciding whether or not to consent to treatment, was under *no* absolute obligation to prolong the patient's life regardless of the circumstances or the quality of patient's life. Medical treatment, including artificial feeding and the administration of antibiotic drugs, *could* lawfully be with held from an insensate patient with no hope of recovery even when it was known that the result would be that the patient would shortly thereafter die. This was subject to the *proviso* that responsible and competent medical opinion was of the view that it would be in the patient's best interests not to prolong his life, by continuing that form of treatment, because such continuance was futile and would not confer any benefits on him.

That was to be contrasted with euthanasia, ie by means of positive steps to end a patient's life such as administering a drug to bring about his death. That was *unlawful*.

Per Lord Browne-Wilkinson:

In these circumstances it is perfectly reasonable for the responsible doctors to conclude that there is no affirmative benefit to Anthony Bland in continuing the invasive medical procedure necessary to sustain his life. Having so concluded, they are neither entitled nor under a duty to continue such medical care. Therefore they will not be guilty of murder if they discontinue such care ... The discontinuance of life support will also be lawful under civil law.

Frenchay NHS Trust v S (1994)

S, a healthy young man, took a drug overdose which resulted in brain damage, he was in a permanent vegetative state. He was fed through a gastrostomy tube through the stomach wall; later the tube became detached and it was not practicable to re-insert it. Hospital was faced with an acute problem: doing nothing, leaving patient to die or performing a further operation. Consultant in charge of S recommended that it was in S's best interests to do nothing and for S to be allowed to die naturally. Judge granted hospital the authority so to do.

Held (CA) that there was no reason to question the conclusion of the consultant.

Appeal by Official Solicitor dismissed.

Airedale applied.

Re C (1994)

By an originating summons C, a patient confined to Broadmoor Hospital, sought an injunction restraining the defendants from amputating his right leg, in the present and the future, without his express written consent. C was a 68 year old patient suffering from paranoid schizophrenia; he developed gangrene in a foot during his confinement and was removed to a general hospital; consultant surgeon diagnosed that he was likely to die imminently if the leg were not amputated below the knee. C refused to consider amputation – he said he would rather die with two feet than live with one. Surgeon made it plain that he was not prepared to amputate without C's unequivocal consent.

Held High Court could, by exercising its inherent jurisdiction:
(1) rule by way of injunction or declaration that an individual is capable of refusing or consenting to medical treatment;
(2) determine the effect of a purported advance directive as to the future medical treatment.

Per Thorpe J:

I am completely satisfied that the presumption that C has the right of self determination has not been displaced. Although his general capacity is impaired by schizophrenia, it has not been established that he does not sufficiently understand the nature, purpose and effects of the treatment he refuses. Indeed, I am satisfied that he has understood and retained the relevant treatment information, that in his own way he believes it, and that in the same fashion he has arrived at a clear choice.

A declaration was made accordingly.

Q Intrepid was thrown off his motor cycle and broke his leg; complications set in and his surgeon wished to amputate to safeguard his life. Intrepid refused to consent as football was his life. Advise the surgeon. Would it make any difference if Intrepid were deeply unconscious from the accident?

21.8.2 Driver and passenger

Mere knowledge that a driver is under the influence of drink does not prevent the passenger from recovering damages should the driver be negligent

Dann v Hamilton (1939)
Plaintiff, knowing that the driver of a car was under the influence of drink, nevertheless chose to travel by the car; she was injured in an accident caused by the drunkenness of the driver. Defendant raised the defence of *volenti*.

Held that the plaintiff did *not* by entering the car, with the knowledge that, through drink, the driver had materially reduced his capacity for driving safely, impliedly consent to absolve the driver from liability for any *subsequent* negligence on his part.

Per Asquith J:

There may be cases in which the drunkenness of the driver at the material time is so extreme and glaring that to accept a lift from him is like engaging in an intrinsically and obviously dangerous occupation ... I find as a fact that the driver's degree of intoxication fell short of this degree. I therefore conclude that the defence fails and the claim succeeds.

Note ————————————————————————————————
In this case contributory negligence, which at the time, *would* have been a complete defence if successful, was not pleaded despite trial judge's invitation so to do.

Owens v Brimmell (1976)
Passenger accepted a lift from a driver who had, to the passenger's knowledge, been drinking heavily; contributory negligence *was* pleaded and was successful to the extent of 20%.

Morris v Murray (1990)
Plaintiff met deceased at a public house and drank with him for some hours; deceased suggested that they go for a joyride in his light aircraft. Plaintiff assisted in preparing for take off and the defendant piloted aircraft; he took off down wind and uphill, a dangerous manoeuvre; weather conditions were poor and club flying had been suspended.

Aircraft just managed to get air borne and shortly afterwards crashed, killing pilot and seriously injuring the plaintiff. Autopsy showed pilot's blood alcohol level was more than three times the legal limit for driving motor vehicles. Trial judge awarded the plaintiff £130,900 damages.

Held (CA) claim barred by the defence of *volenti non fit injuria*. A passenger who appreciated the risk he was taking in embarking on a joyride with a pilot whose drunkenness was so extreme and so glaring, that to go on a flight was like engaging in an intrinsically and obviously dangerous operation, was barred by the *volenti* defence from a claim for damages for personal injuries caused by pilot's negligence; in such circumstances the passenger had impliedly *waived* his right to damages. Although the plaintiff was himself drunk, he was *aware* of the risk he was taking.

Per Fox LJ:

> Considerations of policy do not lead me to any different conclusion. *Volenti* as a defence has, perhaps, been in retreat during this century, certainly in relation to master and servant cases. It might be said that the merits could be adequately dealt with by the application of contributory negligence rules. The judge held that the plaintiff was only 20% to blame (which seems to me to be too low) but if that were increased to 50% so that the plaintiff's damages were reduced by half, both sides would be substantially penalised for their conduct. It seems to me, however, that the wild irresponsibility of the venture is such that the law should not intervene to award damages and should leave the loss where it falls. Flying is intrinsically dangerous and flying with a drunken pilot is great folly. The situation is very different from what has arisen in motoring cases.

Q Toad has several recent convictions for speeding. He offers a lift to Rat who accepts. Toad drives too fast and Rat is injured when the car fails to take a bend. Advise Rat.

Q Brahms and Liszt have been drinking together all afternoon. Brahms offers Liszt a lift home. Prudence, the barmaid tells Liszt to take a taxi; he rejoins: 'What will be will be'. Within half a mile of leaving Brahms hits a lamp post and is killed and Liszt is injured. Prudence on her way home is devastated by the scene. Advise the parties.

At common law a driver could exempt himself from liability by a suitably drafted notice, provided this was drawn to the attention of the passenger who accepted it

Buckpitt v Oates (1968)

Defendant affixed to dashboard in front of passenger seat a notice: 'Passengers travel in this vehicle at their own risk'; the plaintiff had been present when this notice had been affixed.

Held that the plaintiff had agreed to exempt the defendant from the duty of care which otherwise he would have owed.

However Road Traffic Act 1972 s 143 required that a compulsory policy of insurance in respect of third parties should include *passengers*. By s 148(3) the fact that a person so carried had willingly accepted as his the risk of negligence on the part of the user should *not* be treated as negativing any such liability of the user. Thus a notice of exemption no longer has any legal force.

The reasoning was as insurance companies now cover passenger risk and receive a proportionate premium therefor, there should be no argument as to whether or no they were on risk. See now, to the same effect, Road Traffic Act 1988 s 149(3).

The relationship between learner driver and instructor

Nettleship v Weston (1971)

Plaintiff was instructing the defendant, a learner driver; whilst taking a corner at a slow speed she collided with a lamp post and injured the plaintiff, her friend; he had been assured by the defendant that her insurance covered him. The Court of Appeal were unanimous that the plaintiff could recover damages but differed in their reasoning. Only Lord Denning supported *Dann v Hamilton*; he held that the standard of care required of a learner driver was the *same* as that of any other car driver and the same duty was owed to every passenger in the car, including an instructor. For the defence of *volenti* to succeed, knowledge of the risk of injury was not enough nor was a willingness to take the risk of injury; nothing would suffice short of an agreement *to waive any claim for negligence*. It was clear from the enquiries regarding insurance, that the plaintiff had *not* agreed to waive any claim for injury that might have befallen him.

Salmon LJ thought *Dann v Hamilton* was incorrectly decided; the solution he preferred was one of 'special relationship' between instructor and learner. However, on the facts, the enquiry regarding insurance *altered* the special relationship and therefore the defendant *had* accepted responsibility for any injury to the plaintiff.

Megaw LJ also thought that *Dann v Hamilton* was incorrectly decided but did not think that inexperience could alter driver's standard of care.

Q Flapper is about to take her driving test for the tenth time. Optimist is her friend and he agrees to accompany her on a practice run. They meet a runaway lorry driven by Brute. Flapper closes her eyes in panic, and lorry and car collide. All parties are injured in the crash. Advise them

21.8.3 Defences of *volenti* and *ex turpi causa* sometimes linked

Kirkham v Chief Constable of Greater Manchester Police (1990)

Plaintiff was widow of John Kirkham who committed suicide at Risley Remand Centre whilst on remand. Action was pursued against police and not the prison authorities because police were well aware of deceased's suicidal tendencies; they failed to pass on this information to the prison authorities; if they had then the probability was that he would have been placed on the hospital wing on arrival at Risley instead of an ordinary cell; probability was that his suicide would then have been prevented. Police accepted that they should have filled in relevant form advising prison authorities that the prisoner presented an exceptional risk. Defendant argued that failure to fill in the form was a pure omission.

Held (CA) that common law frequently imposed liability for a pure omission where the defendant was under a duty to act or speak.

Per Lloyd LJ:

> In the present case I have no difficulty in holding that the police assumed certain responsibilities towards Mr Kirkham when they took him into custody, and in particular assumed a responsibility to pass on information which might well affect his well being when he was transferred from their custody to the custody of the prison authorities ... As for causation it would have been sufficient for the plaintiff to show that the failure to inform prison authorities materially increased the risk of Mr Kirkham making a successful suicide attempt. *McGhee v NCB* (1972).

The Court of Appeal held that *volenti* was no defence.

Per Lloyd LJ:

> But in the present case Mr Kirkham was not of sound mind ... he was suffering from clinical depression ... Having regard to his mental state, he cannot, by his act, be said to have waived or abandoned any claim arising out of his suicide.

Per Farquharson:

> Defence of *volenti non fit injuria* is inappropriate where the act of the deceased relied on is the very act which the duty cast on the defendant required him to prevent.

Ex turpi causa non oritur actio was rejected by the Court of Appeal as a defence. It was not available where there was medical evidence that the suicide was not in full possession of his mind. The circumstances of the case were such that to afford relief would not shock the ordinary citizen. The Suicide Act 1961 was symptomatic of a change in public attitude to suicide generally and the courts had twice awarded damages following suicide.

Pitts v Hunt (1990)

Plaintiff, 18, and friend, 16, spent the evening drinking before setting home on friend's motor cycle with the plaintiff on pillion. The plaintiff knew friend, the defendant, was unlicensed and uninsured; the plaintiff incited the defendant to drive too fast, intimidating members of the public. Motor cycle crashed into oncoming car, the plaintiff was severely injured and driver killed; his alcohol blood level was twice the legal limit. Plaintiff sued the personal representative of the deceased and also driver of the oncoming car who was exonerated by trial judge.

Held that the plaintiff could not succeed against deceased because they were engaged on a joint illegal enterprise – *ex turpi causa non oritur actio*. Further, *volenti would* have defeated claim but for RTA 1972 s 148(3).

The Court of Appeal dismissed the plaintiff's appeal.

Held that where one person was injured as the result of the actions of another while they were engaged in a joint illegal enterprise, the issue whether *ex turpi non causa oritur actio* barred his claim was to be determined not according to whether there was any moral turpitude involved in the joint alleged illegal enterprise. The issue was, whether the conduct of the person seeking to base his claim on the unlawful act and the character of the enterprise, were such that it was impossible to determine the appropriate standard of care, because the joint illegal enterprise had *displaced* the ordinary standard of care. Since the plaintiff had played a full part in encouraging motor cyclist to commit offences, the plaintiff ought not to be permitted to recover damages for his injuries.

Per Beldam LJ:

> I would hold that the plaintiff is precluded on the grounds of public policy from recovering compensation for the injuries which he sustained in the course of the very serious offences in which he was participating.

Per Dillon LJ:

> On the wording (of the statute) the fact that the plaintiff has willingly, *volens*, accepted as his the risk of negligence on the part of the deceased cannot be treated as negativing the liability of the deceased, and the defence of volenti cannot apply ... For relief to be denied on the ground of the illegality, the circumstances of the joint illegal venture in the course of which the accident, which caused the plaintiff's injuries occurred, must be such as to *negate*, as between the two of them, any ordinary standard of care.

Per curiam. In the context of a plea of contributory negligence, it is logically insupportable to find that a plaintiff was 100% contributorily negligent [as trial judge had done] since the premise on which s 1 of the Law Reform (Contributory Negligence) Act 1945 operates is that there is fault on the part of *both* parties which has caused the damage and that the responsibility must be shared according to the apportionment of liability.

21.8.4 Sporting events

There may be a special relationship between spectator and competitor

Woolridge v Sumner (1962)

The Court of Appeal *held* that the owner of a horse was not liable when it knocked down the plaintiff in the course of a show jumping competition. Plaintiff was not a volunteer merely by standing somewhere near the track; the argument was simply that, in the circumstances, the defendant has not been negligent and could not be blamed for going too wide round a corner, and colliding with the plaintiff.

Per Sellers LJ:

The relationship of spectator and competitors is a special one as I see it, as the standard of conduct of the participant, as accepted and expected by the spectator, is that which the sport permits or involves. The *different* relationship involves its own standard of care.

Per Diplock LJ:

The matter has to be looked at from the point of view of the reasonable spectator as well as the reasonable participant; not because of the maxim *volenti non fit injuria*, but because what a reasonable spectator would expect a participant to do without regarding it as blameworthy is as relevant to what is reasonable care as what a reasonable participant would think was blameworthy conduct in himself.

Thus spectators by their presence take the *physical* risk of danger but do not consent to acts of negligence. However, their presence is implied consent to the competitors to take some risks and this implied consent operates to lower the *standard* of care owed to them, *not* to provide a defence of *volenti*.

Per Diplock LJ:

If in the course of a game or competition at a moment when he really has not time to think, a participant takes a wrong measure, he is not to be held guilty of negligence.

Wilks v Cheltenham Home Guard Motor Cycle Club (1971)

Plaintiff was a spectator at a scramble organised by D1; during a race, a competitor, D2, left the course and went into the spectators; trial judge had exempted D1 but held D2 liable in damages. There was no appeal by the plaintiff against the first finding but D2 appealed.

Held (CA) D2 not liable; on the facts there was no evidence of negligence or excessive speed.

Per Lord Denning MR:

A competitor must use reasonable care – in a race a reasonable man would do everything he could to win, but he would not be foolhardy. In a race the rider is, I think, liable if his conduct is such as to evince a reckless disregard of the spectators' safety – in other words if his conduct is *foolhardy*.

Occupiers' liability

White v Blackmore (1972)

Deceased was a competitor at a 'jalopy' meeting, a car collided with a safety rope; as a result of negligence in the staking of the rope, deceased was catapulted into the air and died from his injuries. At the entrance and around the track were notices absolving organisers from liability for accidents 'howsoever caused to spectators'.

Held (CA) that *volenti* did not apply for the person killed did not willingly accept the risks arising from the organisers' failure to take reasonable precautions – deceased was quite *unaware* that the defendant had been negligent. However the Court of Appeal, by a majority, went on to hold that the defendant had effectively excluded its liability, as they were entitled to do, under Occupiers' Liability Act 1957 s 2(1)

Possibly this exclusion in *White v Blackmore* has now itself been excluded by the Unfair Contract Terms Act 1977 s 2(1).

Simms v Leigh Rugby Club (1969)

Plaintiff was playing in a rugby league football match and fractured his leg; he alleged that the fracture was caused by being thrown against a concrete barrier 7'3" from the touch line; the barrier complied with the bylaws of the governing body of the game which provided that there should be a distance of 7' from the touch line to the ring side.

Held that *volenti was* a defence as footballers who went to the Leigh ground went willingly accepting the risks that arose from playing the game under the rules of the league on a ground approved by the league.

Per Wrangham J:

The risk of breaking one's leg in a tackle is one of the risks which is quite inseparable from the game played under Rugby League Football Rules.

The defence of *volenti* is expressly recognised by the Occupiers' Liability Act 1957 s 2(5).

Competitors' duty of care not to injure each other

Condon v Basi (1985)

Plaintiff was tackled by the defendant in a soccer match; the plaintiff's leg was broken and the defendant was sent off by referee for a serious foul. The county court judge found the defendant to be negligent and awarded the plaintiff £4,900 in damages. The Court of Appeal dismissed the defendant's appeal.

Held participants in competitive sport owe a duty of care to each other to take all reasonable care, having regard to the particular circumstances in which the participants are placed. If one participant injures another he will be liable in negligence for damages at the suit of the injured participant if it is shown that he failed to exercise the degree of care appropriate in all the circumstances or that he acted in a manner to which the injured participant cannot be expected to have consented.

Per Sir Donaldson MR:

I do not think it makes the slightest difference in the end if it is found by the tribunal of fact that the defendant failed to exercise that degree of care which was appropriate in all the circumstances, or that he acted in a way to which the plaintiff cannot be expected to have consented. In either event there is liability.

21.8.5 Rescue

***Volenti* does not apply where the plaintiff has, in an emergency created by the defendant's negligence, consciously faced a risk to rescue another from imminent danger of personal injury or death**

Haynes v Harwood (1935)

Defendant negligently left horses unattended; a stranger threw stones at them and they bolted; the plaintiff was a policeman who was injured whilst trying to prevent them from running down children who were playing in the road.

Held (CA), on the grounds of *foreseeability*, that policeman was entitled to recover damages – *the call for help invites rescue*.

Q Why did the plaintiff in *Cutler v United Dairies* (21.2) fail when the claim succeeded in *Haynes v Harwood*?

Baker v Hopkins (1959)

Defendant ordered two workmen to drain a well; a petrol engined pump was to be used to pump out the water; the men were warned not to start work until the defendant arrived; they did start work in his absence. The pump failed and a workman went down to investigate; then the other man went down; neither returned. A doctor was called, and despite warnings from the fire brigade, the doctor tried to rescue the two workmen from the well, now full of dangerous fumes. Tragically his rescue rope snagged and efforts to pull up Dr Baker failed.

Held (CA) that his widow was entitled to recover damages from the men's employer whose negligence had created the dangerous situation; it mattered not that the doctor's action was *premeditated* rather than instinctive; it could not be argued that he was 'too brave'. The workmen's widows were also entitled to sue, action based on an unsafe system of work. Strangely there was only one claim – *Ward v Hopkins* (1959) – and that succeeded.

It is reasonable to attempt to rescue property

Hyett v GWR (1947)

Plaintiff noticed a fire in one of the defendant's railway wagons and was injured whilst unloading drums of paraffin stored there.

Held (CA) that the plaintiff's action was both reasonable and foreseeable; accordingly he was entitled to damages as the fire was caused by the defendant's negligence in the first place.

The right of the rescuer is an independent right

Videan v BTC (1963)

Infant plaintiff wandered on to the railway line one Saturday morning; his father, who was the station master and lived at the station, saw him there;

the father was off duty at the time and the family were preparing for a shopping expedition. At the same time father saw a maintenance trolley on the line, approaching at a fast speed; father jumped on to the line to save his son; the child was rescued but the father was killed instantly.

Held (CA) that the presence of the *child* on the line to be *unforeseeable*; as a *trespasser* his claim failed. However the rescuer of the unforeseeable victim recovered damages for the defendant's negligence.

Per Harman and Pearce LJ:

> The presence of the *station master* on the track was reasonably foreseeable and so a duty of care was owed to him.

Per Lord Denning MR:

> It was reasonably foreseeable that there could be an occurrence of *an* emergency and the driver of the trolley came too fast and without proper lookout; he ought to have foreseen that if he did not take care, *some* emergency or other might arise and that *someone* or other might be compelled to expose himself to danger in order to effect a rescue.

Q Mrs Nothing and her small son Dunne, are in the waiting room of Toytown railway station; Dunne wanders off and plays on the railway line; his mother screams when she sees an approaching train. Fearless is jogging on his way to work; he hears the scream and runs to the station. He is in time to jump down and throw the boy clear but he himself is killed by the train. Who – if anybody – may claim for damages?

Chadwick v BTC (1967)

In 1957 there occurred the Lewisham train disaster. Plaintiff lived near the scene; he went out and helped in the rescue operation; he was particularly helpful because of his small size, climbing in and out of smashed railway carriages; subsequently, as a consequence of what he had seen and heard, he suffered from 'catastrophic neurosis'.

Held that the defendant should have foreseen that, as a result of its *admitted* negligence, passengers would be put in peril; *somebody* might try and rescue the passengers and suffer injury in the process.

Held it did not matter that the risk run by the rescuer was not precisely that run by the passengers.

Members of the emergency services, although employed to take risks, are owed a duty of care

Ogwo v Taylor (1987)

Defendant negligently started a fire by using a blow lamp to burn off the paint on the facia board under the eaves of his house; he caused thereby the roof timbers to catch fire. Plaintiff, a fireman, went into the roof space to tackle the fire; he sustained serious injuries from steam generated by water poured on to the fire notwithstanding that he was wearing standard protective clothing. On appeal the defendant *admitted* negligence and expressly *disclaimed volenti* but argued that the party who negligently started the fire was not liable to a professional fireman injured by the 'ordinary' risks of fire fighting; he argued he was only liable to one injured by an 'exceptional' risk which the defendant could have foreseen and avoided by warning or otherwise.

Held (HL) that the person starting the fire owed a duty of care to the fireman and *was* liable for any injuries suffered by a fireman while attempting to put out the fire *regardless* of whether the injuries were suffered as a result of exceptional or merely ordinary risks undertaken by the fireman.

Per Lord Bridge:

The duty of professional firemen is to use their best endeavours to extinguish fires and it is obvious that even making full use of all their skills, training and specialised equipment, they will sometimes be exposed to unavoidable risks of injury, whether the fire is described as 'ordinary' or 'exceptionable'. If they are not to be met by the doctrine of *volenti*, which would be utterly repugnant to our contemporaneous notions of justice, I can see no reason whatever why they should be held at a disadvantage as compared to the layman, entitled to invoke the principle of the so-called 'rescue' cases.

To be classified as a 'rescuer' the plaintiff must have a real involvement in a rescue operation

McFarlane v EE Caledonian Ltd (1994)

Plaintiff was employed as a painter on the Piper Alpha oil rig in the North Sea, owned and operated by the defendants. In 1988 whilst the plaintiff was off duty and lying on his back on a support vessel, the Tharos, some 550 metres away from the oil rig, a series of massive explosions occurred on the rig. Over the next one-and-three-quarter hours the plaintiff witnessed explosions and consequent destruction of the rig before he was evacuated by helicopter. Plaintiff claimed damages for psychiatric injury. Trial judge had held the plaintiff was owed a duty of care as a *participant* in the event.

Held (CA) that a person was a participant *only* if he were in the area of actual danger *or* came upon it as a rescuer. Held he was *not* a participant; the defendant could not foresee that the plaintiff on board a rescue vessel would suffer psychiatric injury; he could have taken shelter if he felt himself to be in danger. Further he was not a rescuer.

Per Stuart-Smith LJ:

The plaintiff was never actively involved in the operation beyond helping to move blankets with a view to preparing the heli hangar to receive casualties and encountering and perhaps assisting two walking injured as they arrived on the Tharos. This is no criticism of him, he had no role to play and there is no reason to doubt that he would have given more help if he could. But since the defendant's liability to a rescuer depends on his reasonable foreseeability I do not think that a defendant could reasonably foresee that this very limited degree of involvement could possibly give rise to psychiatric injury.

A duty of care may be owed to the rescuer by the person rescued

Harrison v BRB (1981)

Plaintiff, a railway guard, grabbed D2 who was trying to board a moving train; both fell out. Held, a person who puts himself in danger through lack of care for his own safety and could foresee his rescue *was* liable to the rescuer for personal injuries sustained. Plaintiff recovered damages subject to a finding of contributory negligence of 20%.

Per Boreham J:

> It was the plaintiff's duty according to the rules, to apply the brake; he knew it and I think he was negligent in not doing so ... I have come to the conclusion that had he acted as he should have done it is probable, though not certain, that both the chance of his being injured at all and the severity of his injuries would have been reduced. He should, therefore, bear some of the blame for those injuries.

D1 was sued for failure to ensure platform was properly supervised. 'If there was any breach of duty in having insufficient platform staff (and I am by no means satisfied that there was) I am satisfied that it did not contribute to this accident' *per* Boreham J.

D3, the driver of the train was exonerated from any negligence.

Host and owner of boat has a duty of rescue

The Opogo (1971)

Defendant operated a launch; X, a passenger, fell overboard; the defendant backed up launch but failed to get close enough to X; the plaintiff, another passenger, dived in but died from shock caused by extreme cold. The Canadian court held a duty *did* exist on the host and owner of the boat to rescue a guest who had accidentally fallen overboard.

Held the defendant was not negligent to X, his error was one of judgment only. Defendant was *not* liable to the plaintiff; no fault of *his* had induced the plaintiff to risk his life. Defendant's duty did *not* involve liability to a *second* rescuer when the defendant had not been guilty of any fault which could be said to have induced a second rescue attempt.

21.9 Necessity

It will only be a good defence when harm was inflicted on an innocent plaintiff in an effort to save life

Esso v Southport Corporation (1956)

The beaches of Southport were fouled by oil which had been loosed by the defendant's oil tanker; the tanker had run aground as a result of steering failure. The House of Lords held that, be it trespass or nuisance, the oil was discharged to refloat the tanker to save the lives of the crew; that afforded a sufficient answer to the plaintiff's claim.

Borough of Southwark v Williams (1971)

Defendants were two homeless families squatting in the plaintiff's property. Held the defendants' situation did not constitute the sort of emergency to which the plea of necessity applied; the plea of necessity was limited to cases of great and imminent danger where in order to preserve life the law would permit encroachment on private property.

Per Lord Denning MR:

> If homelessness were once admitted as a defence to trespass, no one's home would be safe. Necessity would open a door which no man could shut.

Rigby v Chief Constable of Northamptonshire (1985)

In 1977 the plaintiff's shop, a gunsmiths, was burned out when police fired a canister of CS gas into the building in an effort to flush out a dangerous psychopath who had broken into it and had armed himself. The canister set the shop ablaze. At the time the canister was fired into the shop there was no fire fighting equipment to hand; the fire service was on strike and the 'Green Goddess' which had been standing by had been called away. Plaintiff contended that the defendant ought to have had available a new CS device since the new device involved no fire risk; the defendant had deferred a decision regarding its purchase pending Home Office tests.

Held first that in deciding not to acquire the new CS device the defendant had made a *policy* decision pursuant to his discretion under statutory powers relating to the purchase of police equipment; decision was made bona fide and could not be impugned.

Second, the defence of necessity was available in the action for trespass provided the defendant had *not*, by his negligence, *created* the necessity. Having regard to the fact that there had been a dangerous psychopath in the building whom it was necessary to arrest and since police had not been negligent in not having the new CS device – the only course of action open to the police had been to fire the canister. Therefore defence of necessity succeeded in *trespass*.

Third, there was a real and substantial fire risk involved in firing the gas canister into the building; since that risk was only acceptable if there were equipment available to put out a potential fire at an early stage, the defendant had been negligent in firing the gas canister when no fire fighting equipment was in attendance. Plaintiff succeeded then in *negligence*.

Per Taylor J:

> Necessity is not a good defence if the need to act is brought about by negligence on the part of the defendants. Once that issue is raised the defendant must show on the whole of the evidence that the necessity arose without negligence on his part ... Whether or not the defendant has been negligent *prior* to the occurrence

of the alleged necessity must surely be viewed *as at the time* of the alleged negligence. If by the ordinary criteria of negligence the defendant can show that *at the time* he was not at fault, it cannot be just when the necessity arises to impose retrospectively a higher duty on the defendant.

Q Ready is driving his car along a country road; on a bend he collides with Steady who is motoring in the opposite direction. Steady is badly injured in the collision. Ready breaks into the nearby house of Go. He rips up sheets for dressings and uses the phone to summon aid. On his return Go is furious when he sees the damage. Advise him.

21.10 Statutory authority

21.10.1 When a statute authorises a certain thing to be done, then any harm suffered as a necessary consequence is not tortious

Vaughan v Taff Vale Railway (1860)
Defendant was authorised by statute to run *steam* locomotives.

Held that the defendant was not liable for the setting fire to the plaintiff's woods from a spark emitted, without negligence, by one of their engines, sparks are a necessary consequence of running steam engines.

Jones v Festiniog Railway (1868)
The House of Lords *held* the defendant liable at common law in similar circumstances, but in that case there was *no* statutory authority to run *steam* engines.

Allen v Gulf Oil (1981)
By the Gulf Oil Refining Act 1965 Gulf Oil were authorised to construct certain works in connection with an oil refinery they intended to establish at Milford Haven. Section 5 gave Gulf Oil power to acquire compulsorily land near Milford Haven. In 1967 Gulf Oil built a large oil refinery on the land referred to in the Act and compulsorily acquired land for that purpose and constructed various jetties and railways in connection with it.

Plaintiff lived in near neighbourhood and alleged that the operation of the refinery was a nuisance.

Held (HL) that the preamble to the Act (preamble recited that 'it is essential that further facilities for the importation of crude oil and petroleum products and for their refinement should be made available') clearly showed that Parliament intended that a *refinery* would be constructed on land to be acquired and such authority to construct a refinery expressly or impliedly carried with it authority to *operate* a refinery when constructed. It followed that Gulf Oil were entitled to statutory immunity in respect of any nuisance which was an *inevitable* result of constructing and operating on the site a refinery which conformed with Parliament's intention. Being a matter of *defence*, the fact that the nuisance was an inevitable result of a refinery on that site was a matter for Gulf Oil to prove.

However. to the *extent* that the actual nuisance caused by the refinery in fact exceeded the nuisance which inevitably resulted from any refinery on that site, the statutory immunity would not apply and Gulf Oil would be liable to the plaintiff.

Per Lord Diplock:

> The question is one of statutory construction: does the Gulf Oil Refinery Act 1965 by necessary implication authorise the company to operate on the land that it was authorised to acquire compulsorily an oil refinery on a scale commensurate with the area of that land and the provision to be made for jetties in Milford Haven for the reception at the refinery of crude oil and petroleum products brought there by large tankers?
>
> I cannot think that this depends on the presence or absence of an express authority to 'use' the refinery as well as to construct it. Parliament can hardly be supposed to have intended the refinery to be nothing more than a visual adornment to the landscape in an area of natural beauty. Clearly the intention of Parliament was that the refinery was to be operated as such; and it is perhaps relevant to observe that in *Metropolitan Asylum District Managers v Hill* (1881) all three members of this house who took part in the decision would apparently have reached the conclusion that the nuisance caused by the small pox hospital could not have been the subject of an action if the hospital had been built on a site which the managers had been granted power by Act of Parliament to acquire compulsorily for that specific purpose.

21.10.2 There may be an apportionment of responsibility

Tate & Lyle v GLC (1983)

Plaintiff owned and operated a sugar refinery on the north bank of the River Thames. Plaintiff had constructed a jetty on the river bed; depth of water between main shipping channel and site of jetty enabled small vessels to load sugar from the jetty. Later a second jetty was constructed to enable raw sugar to be brought in. Between 1964 and 1966 GLC in exercise of powers conferred on it by LCC (Improvement) Act 1962 constructed two ferry terminals in the river; terminals consisted of piers which jutted out of north and south banks and were designed to enable ferry boats to carry vehicles across the river. Effect of terminals was to cause siltation of the bed of the river between jetties and main shipping channel. As a result vessels could not approach to load and unload; in order to enable jetties to operate the plaintiff carried out additional dredging. Plaintiff sued for damages.

Held (HL) that the plaintiff's claim in *negligence* failed.

Per Lord Templeman:

I consider that Tate and Lyle cannot maintain an action in negligence because they did not possess any private rights which enabled them to insist on any particular depth of water in connection with the operation of their licensed jetties.

Similarly the plaintiff's claim in *private* nuisance failed.

Per Lord Templeman:

They must prove some private right over the bed of the River Thames before they can complain that siltation of the bed and consequent decrease of the depth of the water constitute an actionable infringement of their *private* rights whether in negligence or nuisance.

The House of Lords *held* the plaintiff's claim in *public* nuisance *succeeded*. The construction of the ferry terminals interfered with the *public* right of navigation over the Thames between the main shipping channel and Tate and Lyle's jetties by causing siltation on the bed and foreshore of the river. That interference with the public right of navigation caused *particular* damage to the plaintiff. GLC pleaded they were excused because they were authorised by LCC (Improvement) Act 1962 to carry out the operations of which complaint was made. But GLC should have realised that terminals might cause substantial siltation; if it had taken expert advice it could have reduced siltation by 75%. Since an alternative design would have caused one-quarter of siltation that actually occurred and since one-quarter of the dredging costs was therefore an *inevitable* consequence of the exercise by GLC of its statutory powers, one-quarter of dredging costs was *not* recoverable.

21.10.3 A distinction is drawn between statutory powers and duties

Department of Transport v NW Water Authority (1983)

A water main laid under A57 trunk road burst; the defendant was the regional water authority responsible for the main. Plaintiff was highway authority responsible for the stretch of road where burst occurred. As a result of the bursting of the main water escaped from it and caused damage to the road. Parties *agreed* that the burst was not caused by any negligence on the part of the defendant. They also *agreed* that the defendant used all reasonable diligence to prevent the main from becoming a nuisance. Plaintiff sued for the cost of repairing the damage caused by the escape of water from the burst main. Public Utilities Street Works Act 1950 s 18(2) provided that:

... nothing in the enactment which confers the relevant power ... shall exonerate the undertakers from any action or other proceedings at the suit of the street authority or street managers.

Counsel for the defendant *conceded* that the escape of water from the main *would* have constituted a nuisance at common law and *would* have been actionable at the instance of the plaintiff if the defendant had not been acting in discharge of a statutory duty. Trial judge had held that the escape of water from the main was attributable to the performance of a statutory *duty* under the Water Act 1973.

The House of Lords *held*:

(1) In the *absence of negligence*, a body is not liable for a nuisance which is attributable to the performance by it of a *duty* on it by statute.
(2) It is *not* liable in those circumstances even if by statute it is expressly made liable, or not exempted from liability.
(3) A body is liable for a nuisance by it attributable to the exercise of a *power* conferred by statute, even without negligence, if by statute it is expressly made liable, or not exempted from liability, for nuisance.

Held s 18(2) of the 1950 Act was a 'non exoneration' clause of general application to undertakers acting in exercise of a power but *not* in the performance of a duty. Defendant *not* liable for the damage in the absence of negligence, ie where the work had been carried out with all reasonable regard and care for the interest of other persons.

Index